T0328541

So You're An Atheist

So You're An Atheist

Now What?

Yuriy Nikshych

Algora Publishing
New York

Library of Congress Cataloging-in-Publication Data —

Nikshych, Yuriy, 1988-
  So you're an atheist : now what? / Yuriy Nikshych.
    pages cm
  Includes bibliographical references and index.
    ISBN 978-1-62894-108-1 (soft cover: alk. paper)—ISBN 978-1-62894-109-8 (hard
cover: alk. paper)—ISBN 978-1-62894-110-4 (ebook) 1. Atheism. 2. Ex-church members.
I. Title.
    BL2747.3.N55 2015
    211'.8--dc23
                          2015009447

Printed in the United States

Dedicated to my beloved wife Nadia

Table of Contents

BEFORE

He lay there, with no wish to get up, since it all felt so pointless and painful now. Jared had been a model Christian all his life: he said his prayers before supper, went to church every week and felt guilty about the smallest things that he assumed would offend Jesus. Now he felt duped, but by whom he didn't know — was it his church that was to blame? But then the pastor really did believe that nonsense. Was it society? Could one be angry at society as a whole?

Late last night, after months of research and soul-searching, Jared had finally said "atheist," as if trying it on for size, for that is what he now was. He could no longer fool himself into believing the nonsense of the Bible, and the entire world suddenly felt empty: there was no afterlife, and his consciousness would disappear with him when he died, so what was the point of it all? "Why should I bother continuing this charade — how can I even be a good person if there is no God?" he asked himself.

Jared finally mustered up a bit of energy and was able to get himself out of bed, but as he started making and eating breakfast, all he could sense was the vast feeling of emptiness inside of him: the beautiful notion of a universe with an afterlife was now gone. There was no "save game" option, and he felt that he was now living in a much grimmer, darker and unforgiving universe.

"Where does one even begin? Without souls, we're just bags of meat and bones, and our actions are pre-determined by the machinations of a random universe — I might as well be a cockroach," he thought. The phone rang. "Oh no!" It was Sunday, and the first Sunday he had not attended church. "Hi, Honey! How are you!? Are you OK? We missed you at church." It was Mom.

What followed later that day was a long and vexing discussion during which our poor Jared was subjected to countless emotional retorts from his parents, such as, "Don't you want to see me and your grandparents in heaven?" and "Don't you see that this means I've failed you as a mother!" The discussion ended when his father joined in and threatened to not pay his college tuition unless he continued going to church and did not start reading at least ten pages of the Bible a day. Towards the end, Jared felt as though he was the bad guy in all of this — how could he be so "selfish"?

Now, totally depressed, Jared decided to go out for some fresh air. As he was walking and contemplating the negative thoughts that had swamped him, it started raining, adding some much needed visualization for how he felt (which would have been especially apt if there were to be a movie adaptation of this). Soaked, Jared escaped the downpour by running into a bookstore. As he stood there, waiting for the rain to end, he decided that he might as well look around. All of a sudden, a brightly-colored book with black bold letters jumped out at him, as if it was there specifically for him. "So you're an atheist... now what?" He picked up the book and started reading.

The reason for this book

Why spend your time reading a book about atheism? Isn't atheism merely the lack of a belief in a god? Today's major religions have truckloads of varied literature meant to increase the faith of their adherents as well as to gain new converts. Up until very recently, most atheism-related literature was uncommon, obtuse, boring, and laden with other agendas and ideologies.

The past decade, however, has seen an explosion in atheist literature which has helped more and more people reject superstition and begin to actually think. However, these books seem to mostly share the same purpose: to de-convert the person reading it, and to criticize religion. Indeed, it is due to such fine works as *The God Delusion* by Richard Dawkins that I am now free from the corrupting virus that is "faith." I also have read the Bible, Quran, The Book of Mormon, The Bhagavad-Gita and others, in order to get a fuller understanding of the premises of our major religious and spiritual traditions. However, this book is not written for believers, or even those who are questioning their faith. There are plenty of impressive works out there that are aimed at theists.

Rather, this book is for atheists, especially those who have recently lost their faith. How do you talk to believers? Where do atheists get their morals from? How do you "let go" of the emotional scars of religion? Perhaps you need a primer on the arguments that believers might use against you? How do you find meaning in life? (Hint: it's up to you). This book offers answers to these and other questions that newcomers to atheism might experience.

These answers were not somehow magically created by me. I drew on the work of an army of freethinkers who came before, and I have made an effort to distill the essence of their wisdom in these pages. If you read this book and find just one new argument, just one new thought that you previously were not aware of, and think, "Wow, I've never thought of things that way!" then I'll consider this book a success.

This book wouldn't be complete without a briefing on some of the more preachy sects/religions of the United States, including those of mainstream Christianity, Jehovah's Witnesses, Mormonism and also Islam, as well as answers to their common religious arguments. I deliberated over whether or not I should add information about many other religions, but decided that such a task is too great for a single book and unnecessary to the goal I'm trying to achieve.

This book is not a "definitive guide" — it is merely a starting point. Many of the chapters offer "Additional Resources" at the end, listing books and websites you can visit should you find the topic interesting and want to continue your research. Do not feel bound to read every chapter — use this book as a reference manual to get answers to the topics that particularly interest you, and skip over material that you feel you already know enough about. This book is here to help you, not to burden you.

What Are Religions?

Before one can begin to discuss atheism, which is the rejection of theistic claims, one has to digress and reflect for a minute on what religions are. This may seem unnecessary at first — we know so much about them — from personal experience, to movies, to documentaries. If we go by the definition at Thefreedictionary.com, religion is:

> 1 Belief in and reverence for a supernatural power or powers regarded as creator and governor of the universe.
> 2 A personal or institutionalized system grounded in such belief and worship.
> 3 The life or condition of a person in a religious order.
> 4 A set of beliefs, values, and practices based on the teachings of a spiritual leader.

Okay, we have that, and before you doze off, let's look at the implications of religious beliefs. We'll take a fairly common example for the sake of brevity (no doubt many folks will object and give me their own examples, but minute differences are not important here).

> *A deity(s) exists, and it brings me comfort and joy, and an afterlife, while punishing those that behave contrary to its will. The teachings of said being are contained within sacred texts.*

This is, of course, extremely vague, but if you ask people about their religion, usually, this is more or less what they'll give you. You can find many religions that actually don't have many of these elements — there are tribal religions that have little to say about an afterlife, religions with no holy texts but merely oral stories, religions with no "high god" or even with no gods at all — however, for the purposes of this book I'll focus on the more common religions that we actually encounter day to day.

Atheists are often told that they don't have enough imagination to truly believe. In fact it is the believer who is lacking in that department: I do have the imagination to imagine a reality where in a deity might exist, and that would be mighty different from the one I currently inhabit. Imagine if there WAS a "true" religion:

> You walk down the street: all of a sudden you get a sharp pain in your foot. Having faith, you start praying. After a few minutes of said praying, a glowing orb appears from the sky, slowly lowers itself to a bit above your head, and shines upon you. All of a sudden you feel warm and fuzzy, and the pain in your foot is completely gone. You're also wiser now: you have received knowledge that will help you with your job. The sphere then blinks a few times and zips away. All the while, people walk past you and the sphere and nod approvingly, thinking "now, that is a true believer."

In reality, no such thing occurs. Apart from the occasional placebo effect and the calming effect of prayer/meditation, little can be said for the effectiveness of faith. In a study conducted by Templeton Foundation, a group that is pro-religion and gives out prizes to scientists that say anything pro-religious, no benefit was found for patients who were prayed for, and in fact the only thing they did find was that patients who knew about the fact that they were being prayed for actually did worse, possibly due to performance anxiety. And prayer doesn't heal amputees.

It took me an inordinate amount of mental effort to re-frame what religions are in my mind: society trains us to believe that religion at its core is the "worship of God(s)." On a superficial level, this may seem right, but what is religion actually composed of? Here is a short list:

1. A doctrine, usually embodied in a text, book, collection of books/texts.
2. A social group of adherents.
3. Buildings or locations devoted to or reserved for worship/other religion-related activities.

What seemed revolutionary to me, after my deconversion, was realizing that religions, just like political ideologies, only really exist in adherents' minds. The universe does not hold embedded notions of Marxism/Communism/Capitalism — those are merely human constructs, and religion is no different. I felt especially cheated when I realized this, since what I assumed to be a fundamental part of the universe and reality turned out to be just a delusion that was imposed on me by society.[1]

----

[1] By this I do not mean to imply that I was deliberately deceived in some way — I cannot hold any anger towards "society" since it is, with the exception

Why Do Humans Believe?

While there is no "religion gene," human beings are evolved in a way that makes us vulnerable to strange beliefs.

Briefly stated: human beings possess a variety of faculties which, when combined, make them pre-disposed to accept religious indoctrination as a side effect.

It's very easy use commonly-held societal explanations for why people believe, such as, "It gives life meaning," "It brings me peace," and "I wouldn't know how to live life otherwise." However, these explanations are not truly satisfactory and perhaps open up more questions than answers: "How can it bring you peace if you have a fear of hell?" "Surely you'd find a way to live life without a holy book?" "Surely you could find meaning in other things?" These brief explanations are more like "slogans" that people are pre-programmed to say without ever truly thinking about them or subjecting them to any sort of critical analysis.

Instead of the above superficial answers, let us dive a bit deeper and look "under the hood" of religion and examine it in the same way that one would examine the innards of a watch or of some other complex contraption, to look at the "machinery" behind religion. It is amazing that it is only recently that humans became interested why religions exist in the first place, and it is thanks to pioneers such as Pascal Boyer that we can now begin to answer this question.

Before I go on, it is useful to know about the several intuitive "categories" for objects that human beings possess:

1. Inanimate objects: These can be anything from rocks to trees — while trees are alive they are in this category since a tree is but a static part of the environment — it doesn't plot to kill you.

2. Animals: These can have simple motivations such as searching for food and running away from danger.

3. Humans: We have an entire category all to ourselves — when it comes to other humans, we can have individual "models" of other people. For instance, if you are familiar with someone, you can predict how he or she might react, and how you would then react, and how he or she would react afterwards. This type of modeling was, and still is, crucial for a social species. Humans sometimes expand this category to animals they know well, such as their pet dogs and cats, to whom they attribute human properties.

Indeed, we rely on our in-built mastery of the above categories to build models (simulations) of different situations in our minds, and this happens almost instantly. Say you are shown a photo of a dog, running, and in front of it is a big red ball, and just behind the ball, out of view of the dog, is a

---

of a few devious individuals that promote religion for their own gain, largely just as deceived.

sleeping cat. The "solution" of what might happen next happens in a manner so automated that it "jumps out" at you just as you read that sentence. Indeed, when this system malfunctions, it is called autism. While autism can vary in degrees, the essence is that the ability to model other peoples/animals motives is either damaged or not there at all. In an interesting experiment, young children were shown a miniature toy room, with a toy doll inside, as well as two boxes. A candy or something was placed in one of the two boxes, in view of the doll. The doll would then "go outside," and while the doll was out, the candy was taken out and put in the other box. When asked where the doll would look for the candy once it "returned," children below a certain age would point at the box where the candy actually was — that is, they didn't know/realize that the doll had different knowledge of the world than they did, however after a certain age this ability seems to kick in. In autism, this ability seems to be impaired to various degrees, depending on the severity of the condition.

When talking about why some religions are so successful, and why human beings are prone to religiosity, it is useful to be aware of the following concepts:

Category errors

Humans find violations of the previously mentioned categories of inanimate object/animal/human highly interesting and memorable — for instance: statues that bleed, trees that can hear you speak (certain African religions), zombies (visually human but brute animal in nature, also dead, so bonus points for this one), chimpanzees (animals but with human traits). I will also add toddlers — those things give me the creeps — they are visually human but do not yet possess an actual intelligence, beyond a very simple one — when one looks into their eyes it is hard to determine what stares back — I mean, is it intelligent, is it thinking — is there something there?

Examples in religion:

• The bleeding statue of the Virgin Mary.

• Ganesh (Indian god who has the appearance of an elephant but possesses human intelligence).

• Talking donkeys (found in the Bible — yes seriously, I'll give you an example later, keep reading).

• The Holy Trinity — A mortal man who is also God who is also the Holy Spirit, all 3 of which are separate yet one and the same! Extraordinary!

Hyperactive agency detection

Say you are walking in the woods, some 200,000 years ago. Suddenly, a branch falls and hits your head. After some cursing, you quickly look up to see who threw it, only to realize that it probably just fell by itself. Notice how the "default" was that someone threw it, rather than that it just fell —

that's what French anthropologist Pascal Boyer calls "Hyperactive agency detection." Other examples include seeing some bushes move and assuming it's a tiger rather than the wind — evolution favors those that would rather assume it's something dangerous and run away, and live another day to have kids, rather than those who would think, "Oh, probably nothing," and get eaten. It is this tendency that allows us to see agency in everything, from lightning to the seasons, to the creation of the universe.

Examples in religion:
- "God is all around us; every good thing is his doing!"
- "That door slamming shut was caused by Jinn!" (Jinn are Islamic invisible spirit entities)
- "Which god caused me to fail this exam? Or was it demons?"
- "Was it my neighbor's witchcraft that caused the roof of my house to fall?"[1]

While the above examples are clearly paranoid, this tendency to attribute a conscious "actor" to events rather than a non-conscious cause is very advantageous from an evolutionary standpoint — you'll live longer if you are paranoid and kill a few extra folk you suspect are plotting against you, rather than not really caring and then being killed yourself. While this may be unsuitable for today's societal norms, where killing folk is generally frowned upon, for the millions of years that humans and pre-humans existed this was generally a very good strategy to follow. Indeed, humans are not alone in using this strategy — many animals are easily scared: think of a flock of birds being startled and flying away after hearing a branch fall.

Whether it's a roof collapsing, a storm, or an earthquake (assuming we are scientifically illiterate), it is our instinct to first look at "who" did it and why. Indeed, you can observe this in young kids — they will often complain that it's "not fair" regarding things such as bad weather (so they can't play outside), or an engine that "doesn't want to go," or some other event that is not directly linked to an intention that someone might possess.

Mind-body dualism

Humans have in-built machinery that allows us to simulate what other folks think and to predict their actions, and without this all social interaction would be arduous. Indeed, people in whom this machinery malfunctions exist — they are labeled as autistic.[2] We have simpler models for animals (your pet cat won't plot against you over months — it may however have motives such as getting food and doing other cat-things). We even have

---

[1] Many African cultures still have a very strong "who done it?" complex — if someone gets sick/dies/has a misfortune, rather than merely attributing it to chance the people will inevitably look for some "conscious" cause — often a disliked neighbor, especially if they owe him money.

[2] Autism is a very complex disease with various symptoms and degrees of severity. I do not claim to be an expert on it, and am using the term as shorthand for "social impairment."

models for inanimate objects; however, those are physics-based: you can "imagine" what would happen if a ball was thrown against a wall, or if a bottle was slowly rolling towards the edge of a table — we might not get it right in the sense of predicting the exact position, however the model allows us to form decisions as to how to act regarding the possible outcome that might ensue.

A side effect of having models of other humans in your mind (knowledge that will allow you to simulate/predict roughly how they will act), is that once that particular human dies, the model remains. There is no automatic erase function. As such, when we see the dead body of a person whom we used to know, a certain mind–body duality occurs wherein we may have the sense that we can almost talk to him or her, or we almost expect him or her to sit up and "act normal." Even when the body of a loved one is gone, we can still feel some connection with him through his or her favorite chair, his or her car, etc., and feel that he is almost present in some way. This is why, for instance, people often have imaginary conversations with their loved ones who have passed on, and sometimes can almost "hear" them. And this is why the concept of a soul/afterlife/ancestor worship is present in most religions.

Examples:

- I still can't believe he is gone.
- "He" would have wanted it that way.
- What would the Founding Fathers have to say about this?

Young children's trust in their elders

Before children reach "the age of reason," they are very easy to influence. I had fun with this as a kid myself: It was surprisingly easy to convince younger kids of bold unsupported claims such as "My father is the president." Granted, some kids question more than others, but it is a matter of degree. This trait of "gullibility" in young kids is not there by chance: if, for instance, in our primitive past a mother told her kids not to eat a particular fruit since it was poisonous, the "skeptical" kids who would think "No! What if she's tricking me out of trying something sweet?! I'd better try it!" were not as successful as kids who were unquestioning. This came with a tradeoff, however: whenever your parents or other adults provided you with incorrect but plausible superstitious information, such as the belief in spirits, you would be pre-disposed to believe it as well, and this mound of errors would accumulate over generations, provided that these beliefs were not particularly harmful.

These factors, combined, make humans predisposed to religiosity

Let's imagine for a second that you are a human living in a tribe some 30,000 years ago (the time that cave paintings first began to appear) — you hear thunder. "Who has caused this thunder you think — surely someone must be angry, and this angry guy sure is powerful, since there is no way I could cause such a thunder!" Over time, you notice that the thunder and typhoons seemingly occur after certain common events — such as visiting a specific territory or eating a specific type of animal. You soon began to discuss the "personality" of the person who causes the thunder with your compatriots, and over the generations the stories about the likes and dislikes of the "thunder god" grow more and more elaborate, since the exciting content is remembered and exaggerated, while the boring parts are forgotten.

People strive for answers — we are inherently curious, however when the answers are beyond our reach (consider in a group of homeless folk living in caves some 30,000 years ago, with everything around them trying to kill them), we may soon begin developing intriguing "theories" of our own that describe how nature and the world works — our brains are not "blank slates" — we have many predispositions such as the ones I listed above, so it is no surprise that humans began attributing consciousness to things and events that they did not understand, imagining that "someone was behind" natural phenomena such as the weather, the seasons, earthquakes, plants growing, etc. Furthermore, people really love a good story — over time, these explanations will morph, with the most successful ones (the "best sellers") outcompeting the more lame ones. The fun then begins when you introduce other tribes — if one tribe's traditions tell them to be fruitful, to train as warriors and to subjugate neighboring tribes, you can imagine that that tribe will be much more successful than one where the gods tell the adherents to constantly meditate and gather sticks from surrounding areas to create large fires to honor said gods.

Additional Resources:
- *Religion Explained: The Evolutionary Origins of Religious Thought* by Pascal Boyer
- *The God Virus: How Religion Infects Our Lives and Culture* By Darrel W. Ray, Ed.D
- *God Wants You Dead* by Sean Hastings, Paul Rosenberg

Religion as a Virus

Recently, great thinkers such as Richard Dawkins, Darrel W. Ray and Sean Hastings have begun to compare the way religions operate to the way viruses work, using terms such as "meme" and "viruses of the mind." [1]

Religions, as well as political ideologies and other "group-think" ideas, share some qualities that allow them to spread and become successful, hence the usefulness of this analogy. Religion is not something conscious in and of

---

[1] To clarify, it was Richard Dawkins who originally coined the latter concept, which has been expanded upon and reinterpreted by various authors.

itself, or even a "thing" — indeed, it's best to think of it the way we think of a computer virus, only here it infects not our computers but our minds.

Evolution

Polytheistic Canaanite religion → Polytheistic, Monolatristic Judaism → Monotheistic Judaisn → Christianity

Ideas can evolve — this is why the religions that we see today seem to tug at the heart of some people's emotions, and seem to be really hard or scary to question; religions also seem to provide comfort and a framework for one's life. Religions that do this poorly are not long-lived, and the ideas that survive compete even more, creating stronger versions of themselves. Only the most successful of ideas can win over hearts and minds; however the battle never stops — speciation occurs. There are currently thousands of different denominations of Christianity in the US alone. Some view this as a negative and as proof that no religion is true; however from an evolutionary standpoint this is actually a very natural development. Just as with biological species that became separated over large distances and formed into new species over time, religions adapt to their habitats. Of course, the habitats of religions are not rocks and trees, but human minds, and in different places people have different mindsets. It only makes sense that there should be fine-tuned religions that are successful in those parts in which they exist.

• Religions change over time (adapt) to be more successful in their present culture, or they die out.

• Religions take on characteristics of other religions that are successful, or they die out.

• Successful religions are able to increase their amount of adherents through various means — if they do so less successfully, then competing religions they die out.

• Religions mutate over time causing speciation (new branches/sects/ etc., or even new religions) — this speciation allows for greater variability, and, far from being the great evil that it is made out to be, the splitting of religious faiths into sects is actually a healthy evolutionary process.

Defense mechanisms

Ideologies such as religions have defense mechanisms: I'm sure every one of us has witnessed or experienced a rush of anger once someone questions something you hold dear. It almost seems as if it is not a mere point of view, such as, "I think Coca-Cola is better than Pepsi," but as if it were an attack against your very nature — as if someone was making fun of your mother. If you ever felt that way, ask yourself why, and if it was truly warranted.

For example:

- "How dare you question MY faith!"
- "If you are against the war, why don't you move to Canada?"

I will be using Biblical examples here, since this is what I'm most familiar with, but I'm sure you can find a lot to question in any religion.

Propagation mechanisms

Religions also need to spread to survive: this can be accomplished by making the existing adherents "fruitful" and adopting an overall philosophy that making children is what women are for. It can also be accomplished by converting outsiders to your faith through proselytizing or through forceful means (this last one is no longer fashionable in most parts of the world).

For example:

- "Spread the word of the Lord."
- "And you, be ye fruitful, and multiply; bring forth abundantly in the earth, and multiply therein" (to create new adherents).

When it comes to spreading and propagation, religions are not too dissimilar from viruses, in that they both seek out weakened hosts — it is almost a cliché now to hear of someone converting or becoming religious after the death of a loved one or because of a life-threatening illness. The main difference seems to be that diseases seek out physiologically weakened hosts, while religions seek out psychologically weakened hosts. Furthermore, once a host becomes infected, he can help spread the good news/bacteria even further.

Faith-strengthening mechanisms

It is not enough to merely infect: you want your adherent's faith to remain strong, so the religion must have in-built mechanisms that will keep reinforcing the faith. Many religions require regular attendance at group gatherings, participation in repetitive rites, and frequent prayer to maintain and reinforce the mindset. Some Christian denominations label those that fail to keep up as "back-sliders." The vilification of ex-Muslims in some countries goes so far as to the death penalty for such an "offence,"[1] and even equating atheism with terrorism[2].

Creating guilt is also a great way to keep your adherents coming back: Christianity contains a multitude of "sins" one can commit, many of which are perfectly natural biological acts such as masturbation, pre-marital sex and being gay. Turning these natural human urges into sins creates the illusion that the adherents are "in the wrong" against God when they inevitably slip up. This is just as absurd as prohibiting folks from going to the toilet since it is vile and dirty, and expecting them to be sorry afterwards for being vile biological life forms. The Hawaiians, for instance, used to have a variety of strong food prohibitions: it was taboo to eat certain foods at inappropriate times of day, and so forth. This guilt thing is deviously clever however:

- From the believer's standpoint:
  The believer has been bad/weak and trespassed against his God(s) and must now ask for forgiveness.

- What actually happens:
  The adherent is trapped in a "junkie–drug dealer" type of

[1]http://en.wikipedia.org/wiki/Discrimination_against_atheists
[2]http://americanhumanist.org/news/details/2014-04-saudi-arabias-new-law-defines-atheism-as-terrorism-b

relationship with his faith: whenever he "slips up," his only recourse is to go back to his church and repent — this is the only way to absolve oneself of the guilt and feel good. However, this relief is only temporary — eventually he will again "sin" in one way or another, and will require an additional dose of "faith." However, it is the religion that caused him to feel bad about himself in the first place, and the only way to escape this cycle is to free yourself from religion.

Compartmentalization also occurs as part of the faith-strengthening mechanism: perfectly rational and skeptical persons will block questions of faith from those faculties, allowing bizarre and unproven ideas to remain blissfully unquestioned.

Useful parts

It is improper to suggest that religion is "all bad." Some of the concepts in religion are actually pretty useful. For instance, we have the community-building aspect of religion that churches/mosques/temples provide. This was invaluable in earlier times and remains an important factor, in that a strong shared religion can mean a strong and united state, and religions can also encourage acts of kindness, charity and selflessness that can be of crucial assistance to people in need — albeit such generosity is usually (not always) directed towards members of the same faith or community. Religion has given rise to great art, architecture and music, while prayer and meditation can help calm the nerves and provide hope.

One could of course argue that everything useful that religion provides can be accomplished without religion, and that everything that is accomplished through religion is not accomplished by the interventions of gods but due to human effort — and that religion merely "takes credit" for good things that humans do. Atheists are certainly among the funders and participants in charitable and cultural organizations, though I have no statistics on that.

As a sort of "atheist control group" to be compared to the "great" religions, one could perhaps look at Buddhists.[1]

Harmful parts

Before speaking of "harm," one should define whom this harm is directed against — if we look at a single religious human being, we should find at least these conflicting interests that make up a single "person."

The DNA's Interest — here the goal is simple, to pass on your genes, no matter the material cost. If it shortens your life and makes you poor, so be it.[2]

The "Self" Interest — this is what we usually refer to when we talk about our own individual goals. For instance, the paradox we see in humans is that we can choose to override our natural desires and not have kids — I know of no other animal that can make that choice. [3]

---

[1] Many branches of Buddhism are atheistic.

[2] The DNA itself is not conscious — it is but a molecule. However, it is selected for in such a manner so as to create human beings (and other animals) that have a strong desire to have kids. Humans are the only known species that can consciously choose to override this desire.

[3] Many animals, such as ants, have armies of celibate workers that will never reproduce — however this is not a "choice" per se — they did not sit around

---

The Societal Interest — this includes your family, community, political and religious affiliation. At the extreme, we may choose to give up our DNA and self-interest in favor of societal expectations. Heroes, monks and martyrs are great examples.

When it comes to religion, there is always a conflict of interest between what is useful to the individual and what is good to the religion as a whole. Ideally, a religion would "want" you to abandon all "frivolities of life and sin" and devote all your time in service of your faith — however, the danger that this gives rise to in modern times is that the religion will be seen as too extreme or old fashioned, and as such might be abandoned altogether. In modern times religions have to strike a balance between being demanding enough so as to keep their adherents' attention, yet not extreme enough either so as not to alienate them.

Things that are highly harmful to the individual and have no benefit to the religion are usually short lived: for instance, when a mother in the US killed her children so that they would go to heaven, this was widely condemned. Of course, we also have a lot of other "baggage" in the form of sexism, racism and slavery, to mention but a few issues where religion did little to protect us. Luckily, because people now generally find such concepts unfashionable, religious passages that contain references to them are being "interpreted away" or downright ignored.

I cannot end this chapter without mentioning circumcision — I argue that the core benefits are not medical but societal: the hidden role of circumcision is creating a "high cost of entry" into the clubs of those religions which practice it. Studies have shown that whenever there is a high cost of entry people are usually much more loyal and value their membership more; this is like the ritual of hazing in American university fraternities, and of the ritual of the Satere-Mawe people of Brazil, where in order to become a warrior you have to put on a glove made of leaves full of ants that have very painful stingers for a full 10 minutes. We simply cannot justify to ourselves that this torture or mutilation of our bodies was "for nothing." Admitting that you were wrong and paid an extremely high cost for nothing is toxic to the ego, so it protects itself by finding reasons why it was a "good decision" so that

and ponder whether or not to be childfree.

you won't change your mind later (such as with a bad tattoo!). If there is one thing that the ego is good at, it is self-preservation. While unpleasant to the individual, these rituals serve a purpose of creating a strong community.

Junk/boring/weird parts

Apart from all the "functional" elements that religions contain, good or bad, there are also a lot of things that are more or less useless to anyone.

For instance, the Bible contains a log of genealogies that may be useful in a historical sense, but appear to have little to do with religion:

> **Luke 3:36-38** - Which was [the son] of Cainan, which was [the son] of Arphaxad, which was [the son] of Sem, which was [the son] of Noe, which was [the son] of Lamech (this goes on for hours)

This goes on for on and on, like the credits to a movie. Maybe I'm being unfair in criticizing this specifically. Of course, somewhere a biblical historian is teeming with rage after reading this, since these genealogies are uber-important for dating the age of the earth (creationists say it is 6,000–10,000 years old) or for record-keeping purposes. My point is that the average Bible-reading believer, seeking spiritual guidance, will find these utterly useless.

There is also a lot of weirdness/silliness to be found in religious texts. For Instance, the Bible even mentions a talking donkey (like the movie "Shrek," but more religious).

> **Numbers 22:28-30**
> And the ass said unto Balaam, Am not I thine ass, upon which thou hast ridden ever since I was thine unto this day? was I ever wont to do so unto thee? and he said, Nay.

Also there was an instance when Jacob was able to breed cattle that were colored in various colors/patterns by placing colored rods in front of them as the cattle engaged in coitus:

> **Genesis 30:37-39**
>
> And Jacob took him rods of green poplar, and of the hazel and chesnut tree; and pilled white strakes in them, and made the white appear which was in the rods. And he set the rods which he had pilled before the flocks in the gutters in the watering troughs when the flocks came to drink, that they should conceive when they came to drink. And the flocks conceived before the rods, and brought forth cattle ringstraked, speckled, and spotted.

This is just a drop out of the oceans — read any holy book of your choice and you are bound to find your fair share. When these weird Biblical passages are shown to someone of a different faith or of no faith, or to Christians that haven't really read the Bible, they will rightfully wonder what this message is doing in a book of religion. It boggles my mind that there are people, to this day, who will jump through logical hoops to explain away any silliness and inconsistencies — this will be discussed in more detail in the chapter on "Paralogic Compliance."

Idea-bundling

This is the "glue" that makes a cohesive whole out of all of the above discrete elements.

Say I were to give you a list of ideas:

1. Eat every day so as not to be hungry.
2. Work hard and honestly.
3. Live your life in such a way that if you were to remember it in 10 years, you would be proud.
4. Paint pictures of me at bus stops in your city.
5. At 5 o'clock, stop whatever you are doing and loudly shout, "Yuriy is the Greatest!"
6. Get regular medical checkups.
7. Don't cheat on your taxes.
8. Have a group of close friends that you can rely on.

If I were to ask you to give me an opinion of this list, you'd probably go through it and find some of the advice completely logical, constructive and "common-sense," while other parts, such as 4 and 5, would be deemed ridiculous and obviously put there for comical effect — but also to demonstrate a point. The problem, however, is that if you or I were to ask an ardent religious person about his holy text, or about a major "list of important things" from that religion, such as the five pillars of Islam or the Ten Commandments, you will be highly unlikely to receive a point-by-point reply like, "I certainly agree with this commandment, but that one seems kind of silly." This sort of grouping forces people to either accept the religious text fully or not at all — and allows the religion to remain whole in a person's mind.

In the past, religions have been more malleable due to the fact that they were mostly transmitted through an oral tradition, which allowed changes to slowly creep in and the idea to "evolve" — a changed word here or a forgotten passage there can do wonders, sometimes. Also, the translation of ancient texts into today's languages allowed for a variety of different interpretations, suited to whoever was sponsoring the work.

With the invention of writing and the printing press, however, once the translations were in place, it became much more difficult to "accidentally" change the doctrine (although "updated versions" abound). Then we have the mental acrobatics called "religious apologetics," where people knowledgeable in a religion will perform logical contortions (akin to lawyers) to make the religious text mean what they want it to mean. Indeed, this sort of "re-interpretation" can have very serious consequences, with many Christians beginning to ignore the Old Testament (even though that is where the Ten Commandments are found). However, such selective liberal-think is harshly condemned by the more "devout" since it threatens the "wholeness" of that religion.

There will be a point-by-point discussion of the Ten Commandments later on in this book.

Additional Resources:
- *Religion Explained: The Evolutionary Origins of Religious Thought* by Pascal Boyer
- *The God Virus: How Religion Infects Our Lives and Culture* by Darrel W. Ray, Ed.D
- *God Wants You Dead* by Sean Hastings, Paul Rosenberg

RELIGION — WHAT'S THE HARM?

It used to be, not too long ago, that having a strong religion meant that your tribe or community would be successful. Alas, these days religion has become a hindrance — a vestige of old times that desperately attempts to remain relevant through adaptation to its environment (think Christian rock music, "hip" pastors and the acceptance of gay rights contrary to prior teachings), and at the same time by trying to stifle change by opposing social changes, the use of contraception, and new life-saving technologies.

It is the latter part, the "stifling change" part, that we have to worry about. I would be more than content if the fundamentalist religious folk followed the example of the Amish and moved into their own separate community, where they could reject anything new and potentially threatening while at the same time not causing any harm to the rest of us. I would applaud such moves. However, many religious groups today are highly evangelical and they seek to inculcate new members through proselytizing, as well as attempting to make changes to national political systems. Basic scientific discoveries have been held back enormously by religious authorities because they interfered with their dogma, with those who dared to question being subjected to horrendous punishments and execution.

Today, one of the biggest challenges that Christendom causes is the opposition to contraception, which, especially in the African continent, causes an abhorrent amount of unnecessary STDs and unwanted pregnancies. At the same time, US politicians suggest we not worry about global warming since "the end times are near anyway."[1] With such skewed information,

---

[1] Granted, the Oil and Automotive lobby groups have something to do with that as well.

the world is in a great peril indeed, and the great misinformation efforts of religion must be combated with education and ridicule, depending on the situation.

> *Ridiculous beliefs by definition deserve ridicule*
> ~ Matt Dilahunty

The societal problems and suffering that religions cause is a different matter entirely. Countless boys and girls are getting circumcised for no good reason (whether male circumcision brings more harm than good is contested, but there can be no benefit in even the mildest of female circumcisions apart from reducing sexual pleasure, which is only a "benefit" if the point is to reduce women's sexuality). Furthermore slavery, which but a few centuries ago was fully endorsed by both Islam and Christianity, has still not been fully eradicated. The Bible and Quran offer no prohibitions against it, but rather offer advice on dealing with your slaves properly. Sexual repression should not be left out of this list, with countless men and women being made ashamed of their natural desires and made to eschew the potential enjoyment and love they could have had in their lives. Opposition to contraception and abortion alone has made many communities much poorer than they would have been without the unintended children. Teenage pregnancy forces young mothers to halt their education while obligating their male counterparts to find additional sources of income, which in turn takes time away from their studies, sometimes causing them to drop out as well. Religion as an impediment to female rights should also be noted, with Christianity, Judaism and Islam generally considering women to be a cause of temptation and sin, something to be kept at home and controlled as if it where property.

But the biggest problem I see is the entire religious mindset which encourages thinking, "It's all up to God." Instead of taking responsibility for their actions (or lack thereof), people of "faith" may be praying when they could be proactively doing something to solve problems themselves. There can be a degradation of the mind as a whole, since holding a strong religious view generally means heartily despising anything that might potentially bring it into question, and this includes scientific knowledge or basic critical thinking skills, along with an attitude of blind obedience to their religious scripture and dogma while ignoring science and the evidence that's right there in front of you. It is disastrous when this affects even one mind; however, when an entire community thinks this way, we really have a problem. This is one reason why China is becoming the next world superpower.

What True Belief Would Look Like

The Judeo-Christian-Islamic tenets that the believers of those faiths seemingly hold up as the truth do not really correspond with their actions. For instance, let's take the thing that those religions in particular are so concerned about — death. If you are a "true believer," then you should have nothing to worry about — after all, you will be reunited with the God you believe in. Neither should the death of your relatives be of any concern — they are in a "better place" now. Instead of the mourning ceremonies full of crying, weeping and sadness that are so ingrained in our culture, people should be celebrating due to their belief that those folks are now with God, as well as being filled with envy and hoping that they are next. If that sounds cultish or weird to you, then you are absolutely correct; however, it wasn't me who created those faiths, I am but extrapolating the logical conclusion of those beliefs. Indeed, there was a news story a while back about a mother who killed her children so that they would be in heaven before they've had a chance to sin, even though she would consequently go to hell because of her own deeds. Her actions were quickly condemned by everyone, and it is the norm for such people to either go to jail or to mental institutions. However, if you truly hold the Bible/Quran as the ultimate guide to reality, then those actions are admirable, since she made the ultimate sacrifice — an eternity of torture for her in exchange for the guarantee that her children will have an eternity of bliss.

I will no doubt draw countless apologists claiming that "I have an incorrect interpretation" and that, say, some people are afraid of death because their faith is not strong enough, or that they are truly unsure if their loved ones are in heaven or hell, and that "Christianity would never support the actions of the woman that killed her kids." I can sort of see where they are coming from — perhaps for the believer dying is comparable skydiving: you can't be truly at ease until your parachute opens. This, however, does not explain why death is still universally seen as bad. Imagine what would happen if you were to say, "You have such nice and healthy kids — I hope they die in an accident soon so that they can go to heaven as quickly as possible." As a "true believer," an accidental early death should be the stuff of dreams — especially before adolescence kicks in, since teenagers are prone to doing all sorts of perverse, sinful things and disobeying their parents. As long as the death is not a suicide and you are a believer at the time of death, you should be all set — some denominations are a bit more stringent about aspects such as having to confess all of your sins prior to death, or not being drunk at the time of death (for Muslims).

Then there's the issue of dead bodies and how to handle them: the ancient Egyptian's creed required them to preserve their bodies and to bury their dead with items they could use, and if the body were disturbed or damaged then the person would be negatively affected in the afterlife. This is why pharaohs where buried in lavish pyramids with all sorts of material possessions and even servants (in later periods live servant burials were replaced with symbolic servant-dolls). Why then is there such concern and respect for dead bodies in the Judeo-Christian-Islamic faith? The souls are already in heaven, so these bodies are mere "empty husks" that should be discarded as one would discard trash. Two counter-arguments might arise:

- This is done out of "respect."

    If the dead person is already in heaven and with God, experiencing such bliss that we could never even fathom, then I doubt he or she would care what happened to his old " husk" — it would be analogous to a snake mourning its old skin, or a butterfly mourning the cocoon it had just left. I simply don't buy this "respect" aspect when people claim to truly believe that the soul is separate from the body: if there existed a true heaven into which souls would go, and people truly believed in it, then there would be joy and dancing, and the bodies would be discarded without much concern.

- The Bible commands us to bury the dead, and says that the dead will rise.

    This again is not very well thought through — what about the dead that died hundreds of years ago — will they rise up as skeletons? Will their bodies be restored? What about the folk that were cremated?

You would expect that "true believers" would welcome death for both themselves and their loved ones, and would celebrate it, and be the best equipped to deal with the emotional consequences of a loved one going to heaven. However, it is the atheist that is better equipped to deal with death since he can get true closure and "let go," whereas to a believer this would be considered a lack of faith, and he would forever have to wait to be reunited with his loved ones. I can only imagine how much sorrow this causes, and how this will impede the flow of one's "real" life. Luckily, we atheists are spared from such nonsensical thinking and we can let go with grace, and have a healthy emotional outlook on life free from delusions.

If you disagree with what I've said above, here's a quick thought experiment: find a grieving mother who has just lost her son — approach and cheerfully ask, "Well, aren't you happy he's dead now? He's in heaven, so you should be really cheerful!" Chances are that grieving mother will physically attack you. If she really "believed," she would not be sad and would agree with you, and then lightheartedly talk about other things. Given the amount of humans on this planet, it's possible one could find such people, but they would not be considered normal.

More "moderate" parts of society often decry the "fundamentalists," and the fundamentalists are often viewed as somehow more archaic and backward by those that are "more enlightened." However, all that being a fundamentalist entails is the strict and literal adherence to a religion — if I truly believed that my fate for eternity would be determined by whether or not I properly followed some religious principles, you bet I would be the most vehement fundamentalist you could imagine. When it comes down to intellectual honesty, I have a strange respect for fundamentalists, since they at least put good effort into practicing what they preach.

However, from a perspective of deciding what one truly believes in, the vast majority of "believers" today are somewhere in between secularism and religion — many a pastor has preached that "the masses today do not follow the true path" and that that there needs to be a return to "Christian values" (in other words, the "correct" values taught by the church/denomination of that pastor). While there is no such thing as a "True Christian," since there are simply so many denominations that lay claim on that title, we can see that over the last few hundred years, starting with the Enlightenment, Christianity has been dragged kicking and screaming into the modern era, with "bad" passages from that Bible[1] that were once unquestioned now considered "metaphorical," "applying to the different era," "out of context," or downright ignored and passed over entirely. The more educated, wealthy and scientifically literate a society becomes, the more religion loses its grip, becomes more vague and "metaphorical," and eventually becomes mere symbolism, tradition and history.

ATHEISM, THE SHORT VERSION

Indeed, prior to delving into the reasons for atheism, it is again useful to have a look at the dictionary definitions for both atheism and agnosticism:[2]

Atheism
1. Disbelief in or denial of the existence of God or gods.
2. The doctrine that there is no God or gods.

Agnosticism

1. The doctrine that certainty about first principles or absolute truth is unattainable and that only perceptual phenomena are objects of exact knowledge.
2. The belief that there can be no proof either that God exists or that God does not exist.

Now that we have the basic definitions in order, it is also useful to know that atheism can be divided into strong and weak atheism. Here by "weak" we don't mean that you are unconfident in your logical stance.

---

[1] Plenty of those at www.evilbible.com
[2] Many thanks to www.thefreedictionary.com for allowing me to use their definitions for this book.

Strong Atheism – There is no God

Weak Atheism – I lack a belief in a God

These two claims may seem extremely similar, and for most practical purposes they are, however when it comes to debates this difference becomes crucial. If you proclaim the strong atheism position, this means that it is now up to you to prove to the person that you are debating that there is no God, since that is a claim. When someone presents a claim, the "burden of proof" falls on the person presenting said claim. Strong atheism can be referred to (though uncommonly) as gnostic atheism — meaning you "know" that there is no god.

www.thefreedictionary.com definition:

burden of proof
n. Law
The responsibility of proving a disputed charge or allegation.

This can of course become tedious: Some notions of gods may be easier to disprove than others, for instance the Christian biblical God can be disproved quite easily because the 3 Omnis (omnipotent, omnipresent and omnibenevolent)[1] are logically inconsistent since the problem of evil exists, so if God allows suffering he is either not all-powerful or all-loving.[2] However, vaguer notions of "God" that are defined, as, for example "the spirit of the universe" are much harder to disprove — there is however no evidence for the existence of any such deity, so the person proclaiming that "there is something out there" is the one who has to demonstrate that fact, not the other way round — you are merely not convinced of their existence.

Weak atheism, on the other hand, does not require that you disprove

---

[1] All-powerful, present everywhere at the same time and all-loving.
[2] Some apologists attempt to overcome this by claiming that without evil/suffering there would be no free will, however this raises even more questions like the existence of free will in heaven, since supposedly it cannot exist without evil or suffering, which is absent from heaven.

anything at all — your only claim is that you haven't been convinced that a god or gods exist. As such, it is up to the believer to attempt to convince you and you now have to refute all of the logical fallacies and apologetics that will be thrown against you. Weak atheism can also be called agnostic atheism.

Some people prefer to shy away from the term "atheist" and instead stick to "agnostic," however if they do not believe in any God they are technically weak atheists or agnostic atheists, which are the same thing. It is, of course, their right to refer to themselves as merely agnostic to avoid some prejudice that could come with calling oneself an atheist, however it always helps to know the "proper" definitions and explain them to people so that they know better and see how smart you are.

Additional Resources:
- *The God Delusion* by Richard Dawkins
- *God Is Not Great: How Religion Poisons Everything* by Christopher Hitchens
- *The End of Faith: Religion, Terror, and the Future of Reason* by Sam Harris
- *Breaking the Spell: Religion as a Natural Phenomenon* by Daniel C. Dennett

---

GETTING OVER THE FEAR OF HELL

As Sam Harris elegantly observed, it is wondrous that when people have a fear of hell or of a bad afterlife, it is necessarily the one from their own religion. Why is it that if you are a Christian, that you were never afraid of the Islamic hell — if you were "wrong" as a Christian, you could easily have ended up in the hell of a competing religion, perhaps even one made up by aliens or by a madman who sends anyone at all to hell. What makes YOUR hell "real" and the other thousands of bad afterlives "mere fiction?" People are very bad at this rudimentary "math" thing when it comes to calculating the odds of their afterlife: there are tens of thousands of denominations of Christianity alone,[1] with many promising hellfire and eternal torment for the other "non-true" Christians. What about all of the other religions apart from the familiar Judaism, Christianity and Islam? How can you be certain you are not going to the ancient Egyptian or Greek versions of hell — perhaps the ancient Mayans had it right? Even if a hell of some kind does happen to be real, rest assured that you will go there simply by virtue of statistical probability, since the amount of distinct faiths is so large it's hard to calculate, but various sources go from as low from several thousand to tens of thousands — it all depends on what you consider a "distinct religion."

Even if you were never a church/mosque/temple going believer, the fear that by proclaiming your atheism you are somehow "rebelling" and becoming destined for hell can be quite real to new atheists, even if logically they know it's all just stories. Indeed, I've heard accounts of people having nightmares of hell for years after deconversion. For me, deconversion was quite scary as well, however the fear soon went away. However, it won't go away on its own, at least it didn't for me. I recommend listening to a lot of atheistic shows and podcasts till it does — the "Atheist Experience" and "The Thinking Atheist" are great, and if you are an ex-Muslim check out "The Jinn and Tonic Show" — these are great for building up your confidence with facts.

Additionally, for closure, I did something that I never did as a believer — I actually read the holy books — I read the Bible, the Quran, Bhagavad-Gita, The Book of Mormon and others, and all of this gave me closure. I initially assumed that when reading them I would encounter some good arguments and perhaps have my atheism challenged by the wisdom that they contained. Boy, was I wrong. In many ways it was the worst literature that I have ever read. Sure, some books, such as The Book of Mormon, were better than, say the OT; however, overall it was just gibberish, both from the sense of "wisdom," of which it contains none, really; rather, just threats of hell combined with fear and admiration of the given deity — completely lacking in any sort of intellectual quality that could shed light onto how the mind works and how people can actually improve themselves. And the Old Testament, in fact, is pretty much what one would expect from the Bronze

---

[1] http://www.philvaz.com/apologetics/a106.htm; http://en.wikipedia.org/wiki/List_of_Christian_denominations

Age goat herders we are told originated it. [1]

In comparison, when one reads works written by philosophers, scientists, psychologists and sociologists today, one can find an immense treasure trove of insight into the human condition. I highly recommend the book *50 Psychology Classics: Who We Are, How We Think, What We Do. Insight and Inspiration from 50 Key Books* by Tom Butler-Bowdon. It is overflowing with insights into how we actually think and how to improve ourselves. Other good books to start with are Steven Pinker's *The Blank Slate: The Modern Denial of Human Nature* and *How the Mind Works* — either one will teach you more about the human condition than the Bible.

This theme is explored further in the chapter "Religious Trauma Syndrome," as well as the in the "Counter-Apologetics" chapter's refutation of "Pascal's Wager" and "Threats of Hell."

Getting Over Nihilism

Initially, becoming an atheist might bring a touch of nihilism to one's life — the promised gardens of Eden, the 72 virgins, or reincarnation — all gone. And what's more, you seem to be the only person who realizes this. Initially this really bothered me, and my view of life was of a colorless, materialistic dystopia. It was all pointless — however, that was only at first.

The following analogy really helped me: say you are at a movie theater — being nihilistic would be like sitting through a movie and all the while sulking about the fact that the movie is going to end. Sure, at one point the waves will come and wash away the sandcastle of your accomplishments, and it will be as if it never existed — however, does that mean that one shouldn't build sandcastles? Enjoy the sunshine, I say!

Once you get over the fact that one day it will be as if you had never existed, you can begin to truly value life. It is then that you live without the illusion of life being infinite so that there is no need to "truly live" before you die. This life is not just a "stepping stone" to some grander existence, not a mere inconvenience on the way to untold bliss — this is all there is. Better use it well!

"I do not fear death. I had been dead for billions and billions of years before I was born, and had not suffered the slightest inconvenience from it."

— Mark Twain

It was previously assumed that religion and spirituality somehow make people more optimistic and provide additional psychological protection

[1] The goat herders themselves were, of course, illiterate. It was a pre-scientific society.

against hardships; however a new and more extensive study actually showed the opposite results — while in the short term, religion could provide some relief, over the long run it was the atheists who won out with a more stable, coherent and optimistic worldview.

Depression has been shown to occur when a person feels worthless, and where there is no sense of control — with religion, this is hard to combat, seeing as so much of it these days, including Christianity and Islam, have a strong "worthless sinner" ploy. Indeed, when one prays and has his prayers unanswered, one could easily become even more confused and disenchanted.

On the other hand, by understanding that there is no deity controlling your life, that you are in charge, you can finally get a sense of self-control — instead of reading the Bible for guidance, one can read books about social intelligence, psychology, transactional analysis and on the inner workings of the mind — the amount of knowledge we have today, and the sheer volume of amazing books simply makes the old "holy" books appear quaint and weird by comparison — anything written by the author "Steven Pinker" for instance is far more enlightening than everything in the Bible, Quran and The Book of Mormon combined.

If you are still troubled by the whole "you are going to die and it will be as if you never existed" thing, realize that you didn't actually lose anything by deconverting — indeed, I'd rather rejoice at all the time that I will save not worrying about the afterlife. Anyhow, now you can concentrate on figuring out what actually matters to you, and spend this precious little time that you have on important things, not some weird made-up man in the sky.

Another good analogy is that of the cancer patient. Say you've been given a few months to live. Sure, you could spend it all sulking and being depressed — however, that would be a terrible waste. I'd rather spend every minute possible doing the things I've always dreamed of doing — some of which I might not even have recognized were in the back of my mind! There is literally nothing stopping you (except maybe the lack of cash). Sure — you won't be able to do über expensive things such as having a 100-storey statue built in your honor, but living an exciting and enjoyable lifestyle, if done properly, can cost surprisingly little — last year in Ukraine, where I live, a single skydive cost around $50, which was a very good deal indeed.

A great way to deal with nihilism and depression is to count 10 positive things that you have in your life — be it your job, or the fact that you have access to a warm bed and good food. So go ahead — put this book down, I won't go anywhere, I promise — and count those 10 things....

Feels better, doesn't it?

Dealing With Loss

Surprisingly, dealing with the death of loved ones is actually much more dignified when one is an atheist. One can actually get closure — one no longer clings to the hope of seeing them again or that they are alive in some other plane of existence. While theists may claim that their religion brings them comfort, this "comfort" actually comes at great cost — people live in a state of denial, and no matter how devout they are I am sure this still eats away at them, to some extent.

Religion is obsessed with death and dying, however when it comes to actually being able to deal with loss it is exceedingly bad at it, perhaps by design: the Bible and Quran have hundreds of mentions of the word Death, but the passages revolve around sin, hell and the uncertainty of a pleasant afterlife. Instead of living this life to the fullest, a devout believer views this life as a "doormat" to the next. This type of worldview is not only unhealthy when it comes to personal emotional well-being, but is harmful to society in general: in the US, many politicians for instance oppose protecting the environment since they believe that the end times will soon come, so protecting this planet is a waste of time or a distraction from Satan. Religious folks worry about death in terms of whether they are worthy of reaching the "good" afterlife, and have recurring fears about this, which they assuage by going to church/mosque/temple, which alleviates their fears for a while, however they do not realize that religion itself is the cause of those fears.

Perhaps it is my lack of imagination, but I am at a loss to see how one can find closure after a loved one "passes away" if you still believe to some degree that you will see them in heaven (or indeed, if you worry that there is some chance that one of you will end up in hell). Ironically, this makes leaving religion even that much more difficult, since not only will you have to admit that you are mortal, but also that all those loved ones that you were waiting to be reunited with in heaven have long since stopped existing and are never to be contacted.

Also ironically, I have found that as an atheist I am much less afraid of dying than I was as a believer — I have a certain sense of comfort knowing that it will "all be over and it will be as if I have never existed," instead of the possibility of going to hell.[1]

As a believer you do not have that luxury — whenever you begin to question if there is or isn't an afterlife, that is instantly branded as a weakness that must be overcome, and as such you never go through this process of coming to terms with your own mortality, instead bouncing back and forth between ardent faith and the beginnings of doubt, clinging on to faith the way a child clings to a teddy bear.

Instead of worrying about an afterlife, sin, God, etc., we disbelievers are fortunate enough to have a chance to live life to the fullest, and place family, friends, our self-development, love, and adventure, first. I do realize that those things are temporary, and one day it will be as if they never existed, like a sandcastle being washed away at the beach — but that does not take away from the pleasure of building said sand castle. In fact, this awareness can make every instant that the castle is still standing there even more precious.

---

[1] Due to the sheer number of religions and denominations, it is statistically likely that even if one religion were to be "correct," one would still go to hell due to the statistical improbability of picking that "correct" religion.

Hello, dear reader !
If you have enjoyed this book thus far, please
review it on Amazon. It should take around 2 minutes.
I read all of my reviews.

RELIGIOUS TRAUMA SYNDROME

You've stopped believing, stopped going to church and can now move on to new and productive ventures without looking back. If only it were that simple — religion is not merely an "opinion" that can be corrected: when you are a devout believer, your entire personality is based upon it, and when you lose your faith it's as if a rug were pulled out from under you. Furthermore, this rug wants to prevent itself from being pulled, a "harpoon rug" if you will, that is designed to leave deep scars when you pull it. Some people were lucky enough to have been only mildly indoctrinated or raised in a fairly liberal and open-minded environment, and for those leaving may still be traumatic, but it pales in comparison to what "devout believers" experience. Long after you have logically accepted that you don't believe, the emotional parts of you still need time to "catch up." In my case, this was helped greatly by reading atheistic literature and watching shows such as "The Atheist Experience" — nothing like a good dose of that to get the remaining fears out of your system.

Religious Trauma syndrome is not a single "thing," not a mere a knee-ache; rather it's a big ball of sewage that is left after the drainage pipe of faith finally bursts. It includes but is not limited to the fear of hell, depression (you are going to die and religion teaches us that without an afterlife it would be really awful and life would be meaningless), feeling of worthlessness (you are but a deprived sinner, flawed from birth), improper problem-management (pray for it and it will go away versus actually facing and solving your problems). Furthermore, many other mental ailments may hide under or be exacerbated by religion: psychology is discouraged in many a church; seeing the actions of angels/demons/gods in everything is not labeled as "insane" in some fundamentalist denominations and is instead encouraged; and the general "magical style of thinking" that involves prayer and discourages rational thought is not quite a healthy way of thinking.

There is no quick fix: this will be a long journey, depending on the severity of your indoctrination and your mental state, but you are not alone: there are plenty of recovering believers out there that provide support and encouragement for each other. You need not face this alone, as there are people that have already been what you have been though and worse. If you are currently suffering from Religious Trauma Syndrome know this: you will feel happy and optimistic once more, it is but a matter of time, and you are not alone.

Additional Resources:
- *Leaving the Fold — A Guide for Former Fundamentalists and Others Leaving their Religion* by Dr. Marlene Winell
- Reddit community links:
    - Ex-Christians: www.reddit.com/r/exchristian/
    - Ex-Catholics: www.reddit.com/r/excatholic/
    - Ex -Mormons: www.reddit.com/r/exmormon/
    - Ex-Muslims: www.reddit.com/r/exmuslim
    - Ex -Jews: www.reddit.com/r/exjew/
    - Ex-Bahai : http://www.reddit.com/r/exbahai/
    - Misc: **www.reddit.com/r/Exittors/**
- "The Thinking Atheist" YouTube show

HAPPINESS AS A SKILL

Today's culture is centered on the outward appearance of happiness and self-fulfillment: as long as you broadcast to everyone around you that you feel great, you are perceived as "normal." I'm not here to preach some old adage like "money can't buy happiness" or other platitudes, but rather to suggest to you that happiness — that is, being at peace and feeling good about yourself — is not some "outward" goal that one must accomplish outward feats to achieve, such as having more money, power and romance (although those certainly do help). It is an inward "muscle" that one can train. Research has shown that while there is a correlation between wealth and happiness, it only goes up to a point. If you were previously dirt poor, struggling to pay your rent and feed yourself, and suddenly became a bit richer, you would definitely feel happier. However, once the basics are secured, additional money will bring only "diminishing returns": a million dollars for Bill Gates is not the same as a million dollars for someone who can't afford lunch.

If you are already generally well-off, additional money won't really make you happier, but deeds and actions will. While there are hundreds of books devoted to this topic, I will present to you a core of principles that it all boils down to:

1. "Count 10 things you are grateful for" — instead of focusing on the negative, find 10 things you are thankful for — these can be as simple as having a place to sleep or enjoying a hot coffee. Counting them will make you focus on the positive, and is a great way to get out of a bad mood.

2. Sleep at least 8 hours a day: an additional hour of television or browsing the Internet won't bring any more value into your life. Depending on your physiology, if you aren't getting 8–10 hours of sleep a day you are sabotaging your health (studies have shown that sleeping less can make one more prone to sickness and weight gain), and a worse, you live with that zombie-like mood which both kills your productivity and your enjoyment of life.

3. Exercise: even if you start exercising for 5 minutes per day, you will have better self-esteem and will feel more invigorated.

4. Don't depend on others for your happiness: you don't need society's or some specific individual's approval to be happy, and neither is your happiness tied to the emotional states of your friends or family — if they want to be depressed that's on them, but you owe it to yourself to take care of yourself.

5. Have some quiet time during the day: don't spend all of your free time, especially the time before you go to sleep, watching television or browsing the Internet: take a short walk or read a nice book such as this one, or meditate. You will be surprised how much even 10 minutes of relaxation can improve your life: start simple, and build up that skill.

6. Do not force yourself to feel happy: it is sometimes better to admit that you feel bad, and "feel good about feeling bad," if that's not too confusing — once you feel good about feeling bad, eventually you will feel good.

7. Get sunlight and go outdoors whenever possible: it's great for both exercise and simply seeing the sun/grass/flowers/trees instead of a computer monitor that you are sitting in front of all day does great things.

8. Find other things that make you happy and increase the amount of those in your life. Also, identify negative influences, be it obsessing over the news, junk food, or friends/family with depressed/negative worldviews, and decrease your exposure to them. This should be common sense. Control your lifestyle in such a way that you will become more happy, successful and

optimistic. This takes time and energy to perfect and requires a lot of experimentation, but merely understanding that this is possible and that one has the power to do it is already half of the work.

Additional Resources:
- *Stumbling on Happiness* by Daniel Gilbert
- *The Origin of Everyday Moods* by Robert E Thayer

FINDING MEANING

Meaning, like beauty, is in the eye of the beholder. Religions provide a rigid structure as to how one sees himself within the universe — there are "absolute" laws, ways of behavior, and there is a goal — to live forever in some form of bliss (at least with most). Initially, being an atheist may be disconcerting in this regard — there is no "higher up" person to tell you what to do.

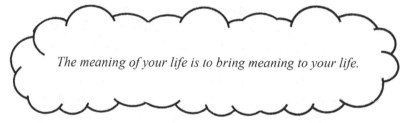

The meaning of your life is to bring meaning to your life.

Before becoming an atheist, I personally just wanted to "get through" life without sinning too much/causing too much of a hassle. However, after becoming an atheist something changed: All of a sudden it was I who was responsible. I could no longer fire off excuses — it was time for a change. What should that change be for you, o reader? It is up to you. However, I will provide examples of how I changed my life.

First off, there isn't, or at least there wasn't in my case, a drastic "sudden" change. Rather, it's about the slow accumulation of choices that are made as a result of the new worldview.

The sheer luck that you are reading this is an accumulation of fortunate events that began a long time ago, starting from your ancestors, who, all in succession, avoided being eaten or dying prior to mating. Treat this life like the finite gift that it is. We've already considered the cancer patient, who is given just months to live with no chance of a cure — what would be his first priority, while his health's still adequate? You, fellow reader, are no different — you merely have a bit more time. The average human lifespan, worldwide, is 65 years or 780 months. That may seem to be a lot, but how quickly did the past month go by for you? You feel as if a week or so has passed, but, no, bam! A month! And forget about the old cliché of "living to 100" — this is actually very rare — in the US, in 2010, only 0.0173% of the population lived past one hundred (for those who are bad with percentages, that's one or two people per every 10,000). The scientific effort to combat aging is speeding up, with even Google joining the fight by launching a company called "Calico," which will focus on health care and living longer, and will be headed by an Apple executive — alas, details at the time of this writings are still very sketchy, so I will not speculate further. For all intents and purposes today there is no cure for aging. I prefer to treat my life as it is — finite and precious.

Oftentimes, I hear complaints that there are no atheism songs. Indeed, I myself assumed this for a while, however it seems that there are actually many really enchanting songs out there. Of note is "Rant" by Bo Burnham, as well as everything by "Mc Hawkings" which, while not atheistic per se, is extremely pleasurable to listen to.

It is easy, with the common availability of online atheist communities, books and videos to become deeply engrossed in the atheist culture and forever have it as one of the core parts of your identity. I, however, am scared of the prospect of growing old and having "atheist" as the thing people would remember me by — if anything, atheism, after you've had a chance to unwind a bit after the loss of your religion (be it months or years), should slowly recede into the background as you begin doing new and exciting things with your life. Writing this book gave me a reason to do an inordinate amount of research on the subjects of atheism, anthropology and religion, and I feel enriched by this; however, I hope that if you find me in five or ten years, I will be interested in something totally new, while still holding my atheist outlook. Atheism can be a launch pad into research in related topics: comparative religion, anthropology, history, psychology, philosophy and science are all subjects that one can explore. Beyond that, it is not an achievement, career, or something to "do."

I finally began doing exciting things — exploring abandoned buildings and even towns — I visited Pripyat, the abandoned city near Chernobyl, started skydiving, and something called rope jumping. It's like Bungee jumping except it involves swinging like a pendulum after the fall. I also started reading more — all of a sudden, I realized that there are many books full of insights into how the mind works and how we make decisions — I couldn't read fast enough.

I remembered that a while back, long before becoming an atheist, I had made a list of things to do before I die — and it actually included some of the above. I realized that now was the time to actually do all the things I had been putting off.

You might accuse me of a logical inconsistency here — I was just talking about how awesome life is, yet now I've begun doing extreme (risky) things. This did puzzle me for a while; however, I prefer to think of it this way: I have an expensive camera that I use to record my rope jumps — sure, the camera might get damaged or even fall off, but what's the point of keeping it safe in a drawer? Indeed, I am now more afraid of NOT taking risks, and being disappointed when I find myself on my deathbed. If I find myself dying in a field somewhere after a failed parachute jump, my last words will be "worth it...."

Our Place In the Universe

It used to be that man knew very little indeed. Think back to before the Enlightenment or the development of the scientific method: humans explained their tumultuous lives as being controlled by spirits, angels, gods and demons, all conspiring and plotting to either make their lives easier or throw in a new round of hardship. Anything from a severe winter to an outbreak of smallpox to, indeed, a good harvest, was explained away as being caused by anthropomorphic "agents" — here I use the term "agent" in the way it is used in Game Theory, that is, as "a conscious entity who performs actions in pursuit of his interests or motivations." Indeed, this way of thinking is what makes us humans who we are — we are adept at seeing patterns. Human beings have amazing in-built wiring, for example, that makes us expert "face detectors" — we can see faces everywhere, starting from actual faces, to paintings, to crude drawings (think of the "smiley face" emoticon), or even faces where there aren't any actual faces — such as the face on the moon. Indeed, apart from faces or visual cues, we are adept at recognizing intent. Pascal Boyer, in his book *Religion Explained*, gives the example of a person walking in the forest. If he were suddenly hit by something on the back on his head, his first thought would be, "Who did that? Who is trying to kill me?" And only upon further thought would he deduce that perhaps it wasn't anyone at all, but just a branch that fell from the tree. This ability to see agency even where there isn't any, was, and perhaps still is, key to our survival — it's better to assume that that rustling in the bushes is a tiger, rather than just the wind — and run away than to be calm and rational and get eaten by a tiger. Only those who assume that "someone" is there survive and pass on their genes.

While useful for immediate survival, this inclination to detect agency even where there is none is one of the primary causes of belief in something "out there." Combine that with plain ignorance and fear of the unknown, as well as the wish to tell exciting stories, and you have everything set in motion for the creation of spirits, deities and demons to control fate and nature — from rain to thievery to earthquakes. Whenever something happened in the world that was of any significance, a deity or spirit was ever-present and in charge of said matter, always ready to be appeased with an offering. Even with the so called "progress" to monotheism, all that changed was that now we were answering to a single authority, rather than many disparate deities, but the general idea persisted.

Be it poly or monotheism, humanity still regarded itself as so important that the natural elements that surrounded them cared about how they acted, what offerings they brought and what prayers they said, and of course whom they copulated with. Surprisingly, the notion that this is belief is actually incredibly arrogant never really crossed anyone's mind up until very recently; or if it did, then those notions were quickly suppressed. To be fair, some ancient Greek schools of thought did entertain the notions that perhaps there were no gods and everything that occurred around them was just due to the forces of nature, however that was just a small drop in a sea of theism, and indeed at the time their opinions were not exactly grounded, seeing as we still didn't have scientific explanations for the origins of life, and, while atheism would still technically be the "default" position, since one would have to show evidence for the existence of gods for theism to be tenable, the scientific method was still in its infancy, and universal literacy was still nowhere in sight.

Indeed, we were literally "at the center of the universe" up until very very recently, though I do have to point out that the notion that Copernicus was the first to discover that the earth revolved around the sun and not the other way round is false. This was known as far back as Ancient Greek times.

Indeed, the notion that atheism is somehow arrogant is absurd. Claiming that you are at the center at the universe and that it was created for you — that's what's arrogant; and to claim that the creator worries about your sexual habits — now, that's just conceited. It is only through science that we begin to realize that maybe we aren't the gleaming jewel of the universe, which is infinitely large — so large that our imagining how large it is, even to the best of our ability, would not do it even meager justice, like an ant trying to imagine a continent and thinking of the next room or the neighbor's yard. But, even if the ant were indeed able to imagine the scale of an entire continent — a feat most humans can't accomplish, unless they perhaps personally did some sort of "trans-continental marathon" — it would still be many orders of magnitude short. The best I can do is imagine that we are like a bunch of bacteria on a speck of dust, floating around somewhere and thinking how very much important we are — and indeed when you take the scale of the universe into account, the earth is just a tiny speck of dust that may disappear or be swept aside without anyone noticing or caring.

THE ORIGIN OF THE UNIVERSE

Many a religious person has deemed science inadequate since "it doesn't have all the answers" to such questions as what was there before the Big Bang, not to mention its inability to proclaim *who* created the universe, and *why*.

Of course, what those people fail to realize is that there can be such a thing as an incorrect question: I may ask "What is the color of deceit?" and "Why is the earth so square-shaped?," but the mere ability to formulate words does not then dictate that if science "can't find an answer" then science is somehow deficient — indeed, it is only by becoming scientifically literate that one may even begin to pose intelligent questions, and hopefully someday even find solutions.

How did the universe begin?

We have all heard of the term "Big Bang." It may surprise you that unlike its depictions in the mass media, scientists don't think that there was an actual explosion, but merely a rapid expansion. Indeed, the scientist Fred Hoyle, who was not a proponent of the Big Bang Theory when it was still new, intended his usage of this term to poke fun at the theory, and alas the term stuck. All of this took place some 13.798 billion years ago (the "Big Bang," not the 1949 BBC radio broadcast where the term was coined). Initially there were but very simple elements, but these slowly began to be pulled together into cosmic clouds (nebulas), and eventually these began to be pulled together forming stars and planets.

Why did the universe begin?

After all — there could have been "nothingness" forever. Depending on whom you listen to:
1. The religionists: God(s) made it happen!
2. American theoretical physicist Lawrence Krauss's explanatory synopsis: Nothingness is actually not nothing: every empty piece of space still has some properties, including being able to transmit light, support the laws of physics. And there are quantum particles constantly appearing "out of nothing" everywhere and that nothingness is inherently unstable — however, each such particle has a counter-particle and they self-destruct so quickly that that no major laws are broken and it's all well and good. Krauss's explanation is that something analogous happened when the universe was created, but the amount of matter was ever so slightly more than that of antimatter, and hence we have some matter in the universe, but not too much (think of the vastness of empty space).
3. String theorist's explanation: "There are some cosmic brain things that rub together and when they collide universes happen. We proved it using maths."

Alas, I'm no physicist and cannot make judgments regarding the validity of these claims or other theories. Not knowing this does not give victory to the believer, since he doesn't "know" either, but rather "pretends to know."

What happened before the Big Bang?

This question is considered incorrect by many, since the concept of time relies on matter: without "stuff," the concept of time is meaningless. It's like asking ,"what's north of the North Pole?"

Whether or not you choose to go by any of the current theories regarding how the universe came into being, "I don't know" is a perfectly valid answer, albeit one that religionists seem to be allergic to: they assume that your admitting that you don't know somehow gives more validity to their own claims. However, even if there was a total absence of evidence on a topic, be it evolution, the causes of diseases, the creation of the universe, etc, the supposed "answer" of a religious person would be no more valid than saying "magical bunny rabbits did it."

Additional Resources:
- *A Universe from Nothing: Why There Is Something Rather than Nothing* by Lawrence M. Krauss
- *The Elegant Universe: Superstrings, Hidden Dimensions, and the Quest for the Ultimate Theory* by Brian Greene
- *The Grand Design* by Stephen Hawking

REPLACING RELIGION WITH SOMETHING USEFUL

Whether you used to be a devout church/mosque/temple-goer or a plain non-practicing vanilla believer, the first few months or years after losing your religion may bring forth a sort of vacuum: you used to have a multitude of things pre-decided for you, be it your activities on a certain day of the week (going to church, not doing things on the Sabbath), dietary prohibitions (vegetarianism, not eating pork) or the plain old "not doing anything fun" spiel that religions tend to propagate, since fun things are Satan's way of distracting you from worshipping God. It is the opinion of some atheists that religion is similar to a cancer, and that asking what one should replace cancer with is meaningless. I think the reality is much more complex than that, since religion is not merely some ailment that one can get rid of and forget about the following week. It is, in a way, a "societal program," to use fancy computer analogies, that tries to direct your behavior towards its propagation and keep you a devout believer. As a consequence, many behaviors, opinions, tastes and habits that you perceive as "your own" were arrived at through the lens of your religion. The notion that human beings are objective and rational decision makers that we like to bestow upon ourselves (but, surprisingly, usually not upon many of our acquaintances), is but an illusion: we strive for rationality, but are all subject to our cognitive biases, and are tied to seeing things from our point of view. Indeed, seeing things from every single possible point of view would be extremely tedious and downright impossible: you simply could not form an opinion of everything you saw from an atheistic, Muslim, alien and a velociraptor's point of view, to name but a few — and if you did you'd probably go insane.

Instead of being upset about all of this however, why not use this knowledge to your advantage? Create your own "behavioral guidelines" which will propel you towards success (or at least, gradually make you more successful/fit/knowledgeable than you currently are). We are all doing this naturally as is — we have instincts and notions regarding which things are harmful and useful, for instance that junk foods are bad, listening to language-teaching audio books is good. These notions are all floating around inside your head, however to really bring them "up front" and make them a center of your attention write down, say, 5-10 them — on paper (writing them on a computer or a mobile device and never opening them later is not the point), and hang them on your wall. Here is a simple example off the top of my head — surely you can do better:

1. Exercise at least once every 2 days.
2. Listen to several audio books a month.
3. Do something exciting once a month.
4. Do not eat bread/wheat/potato based produce.
5. Remember 10 good things about your life when you are feeling sad.
6. Live life now in a way that you'd be proud to remember in 4 years.
7. Do not eat after 6 pm to lose weight.
8. Weigh yourself in the morning and record your weight.

That wasn't so hard — and there don't have to be many. Indeed, writing down 30-50 would probably defeat the purpose, as you'd never remember them all. Of course, these ones are specific to me, and it is up to you to write your own. The point is that surely if religions have used this power for so long, you can create your own code — one that does not serve some social cause but merely makes your life better and you a happier human being. Human willpower is an exhaustible resource: it may be easy to avoid that bag of potato chips in the morning, but after a hard day's work of doing complicated work and dealing with family you just want to unwind, the depletion of your "willpower resource" makes it much more difficult to "just say no" — be it to alcohol for an alcoholic, or to food for a slightly overweight person such as yourself. However, by using this trickery, assuming you have been religious and have followed religious prohibitions despite what your short-term desires wanted, you can now say "No, eating this fatty food is against my religion," "Watching junk-TV is against my beliefs," "I have to exercise every day — it's my dogma." Hereby, you replace the religion of society with your own "religion" of personal growth and wellbeing. Many people might be weirded out by me calling this "religion" — and indeed it's not, except for as a metaphor — and those things are darn useful. By calling something a "religion" instead of merely "things I said I'd do," you elevate the importance of those beliefs. This isn't for everybody of course, especially if religion has a negative connotation in your mind — in which case by all means find a word that suits you best. You may not even need such a "code" — by all means, if you are totally happy with the way your life is now and want it to remain generally the same, then by all means, keep at it. However, if you want to use those brain pathways that religion once commandeered, and instead repurpose them for serving your own improvement, then some brain-hacking, such as the one I mentioned above costs nothing to try.

Then there's another question: "What do you do on Sundays that you no longer go to church?" Here the list is just endless:

1. Sleep
2. Skydiving
3. Meet new people
4. Learn a new language
5. Go hiking
6. Anything else you want!

If religion contains within it such power that it can send men to war, or give a Hindu holy man the motivation to hold his arm up for 40 years in an unnatural position, causing it to deform,[1] surely you can subvert that latent power within you for something useful such as losing some weight, quitting smoking, or learning a new skill.

BECOMING SUCCESSFUL

Religious people can be plenty successful as well, and this chapter isn't here to dispute that, or to do some tedious comparison between the successfulness of believers vs. non-believers. However, having as few false beliefs as possible and a more skeptical mindset may give you an edge: you for instance won't spend your time praying for success, part-taking in complex rituals or giving money to the church in hopes that it will bring you good luck. Whether it's business, your social life, relationships or some specific skill, there are literally millions of people you can gain experience from — there is simply no need to "re-invent the wheel," so to speak: The thing that allows humans to be successful as a species is the ability to easily transmit knowledge — you simply don't have to do all of that tedious trial and error when you can simply read about it.

1. Read about it. Whatever you are interested in, merely watching documentaries/clips on YouTube isn't enough (though it is a good start). Get yourself a Kindle or an Android-based tablet, or an mp3 player and get as much useful content on it as possible. The amount of audio books these days is amazing, and there is

[1] Just Google "Hindu holds arm up."

no excuse for not listening to them during times when you are not doing anything, for instance your commute to work.

2. Surround yourself with like-minded folk that you admire. We have this almost primal need to think of ourselves as "unique self-determined individuals,"[1] however human beings are inherently social, and the mindset of the people that we hang out with the most affects us greatly. Imagine for instance a gifted child with lots of potential hanging out with drug addicts/losers. Even if he does not become an addict himself, he will have nowhere near the success he would have enjoyed if he'd spent his time with young wanna-be entrepreneurs and people passionate about their talents. Even cops are not immune: a friend of mine, upon hearing my above analogy, commented that he knew several cops who, over the years, had their personalities change depending on their specialization: the cops who performed administrative tasks stayed more or less the same, for instance, while those who dealt with alcoholics, drug addicts and generally the "lower end" of society on a day to day basis for several years acquired many of the traits of such people — maybe they didn't become alcoholics, but their mannerisms became more and more degenerate. Use this knowledge to your advantage — choose your social environment carefully; think of yourself as a gardener that allows the best flowers to blossom, while trimming all the weeds: surround yourself with successful people that you look up to and that you respect.

3. "Do Your Thing." Yes it's a cliché, but people spend most of their lives either asleep or at work. As such, having a job that you find rewarding is the biggest luxury available. Find something that you are good at or are passionate about as soon as possible, and spend your free time and resources increasing your skills in that area — success isn't guaranteed and it won't come at once. The "universe" has no obligation to make you succeed. A job that you enjoy is worth more than a higher paying job that you can't stand — many people just don't seem to get this.

4. Get rid of self-limiting beliefs. It is very easy to come up with reasons why you can't do something:
   - You don't have enough money.
   - You are not smart enough.
   - You didn't start out trying this at an earlier age when you

---

[1] This is true of today's "western" mindset; however many cultures have a diametrically opposing view, stressing ties and "obligations" to the family, community, clan/village/country/emperor.

had more energy.
- You don't have a good-enough education.
- You are too fat.
- You are too socially awkward.

5. Our minds are very talented at this art — if you want reasons as to why you will fail at something or why you should give up trying, you will get countless plausible rationalizations that you can feel comfortable with. The skill however is to realize this, and instead to think of your advantages and about why you CAN accomplish your goal. Let the rest bellow in their excuses.

6. Give yourself permission to be successful. Sometimes, the "last thing" that may be holding you back is a mental block — perhaps you are too comfortable living in your current reality, and changing your self-concept into that of someone who is successful is unfamiliar and scary. When no one is around, stand up and say "I ___, give myself full permission to accomplish ____ and become fully successful." This is not some magical call to the universe, however this is a very useful psychological tool that allows you to mentally transition into that mindset.

7. Of course, doing that in and of itself won't make you successful, but it's a good start.

8. Cut out "Junk-Activities." Just as there are Junk-Foods, there are also Junk-Activities. Some that come to mind include watching hours of TV every day and mindless Internet browsing. Of course, all things may have value in moderation and there is nothing wrong in watching a good show every now and again — the problem occurs when you waste your time that could otherwise have been spent learning a new skill, reading a great book or finding that new job watching reality television. It would take the resolve of a monk to fully cut everything out, so make the transition gradual.

9. Become fitter. A healthy body is important for productivity; exercise at least once every several days. You will feel much better, have higher self-esteem and will feel that you can accomplish more. The exercise will also make you feel invigorated. Sir Richard Branson, when asked about the key to success was, mentioned exercise — your brain simply works better.

10. Have a concrete plan of action. Write down a checklist of all of the things that need to fall into place to accomplish the goal you want. That way, it won't remain a vague notion in your head, but rather it will become an actionable plan that you can expand upon and improve. The biggest impediment to action is not

"lack of willpower/motivation" but vagueness. Be as specific as you possibly can and write down concrete tasks that you can do — make sure they are realistic and possible to accomplish: You want to split them up into as many small "sub-tasks" as possible, that way you get to feel that sense of accomplishment more often, and as a result will feel more motivation and progress faster.

11. Don't be afraid of rejection or failure — society trains us into believing that those are necessarily negative. Instead, treat them as neutral. As the old saying goes, "It does not matter how many times you fall, but how many times you get back up." Most successful entrepreneurs have a lot of failure behind them — many a failed business or venture — that is totally fine, what matters is that you don't view that as "proof that you are unworthy," but merely a learning opportunity that will make your next try more successful. It is but the "common folk" that fail once, get scared and get back into the box that society has provided for them.

12. Skill doesn't come overnight — there is no "quick fix" solution that today's popular culture seems to be focused upon. Studies have shown that to become adept at a particular skill, such as a new language, musical instrument, trade, etc., you need roughly 10,000 hours of practice. Be prepared for a lot of toil if you truly want success, but it will come... eventually.

13. Become job-independent. Remember how happy you were once you became financially independent from your parents (or if you still are dependent, how happy that would ostensibly make you)? You get a lot more freedom and can choose to spend your money the way you wish. Becoming job independent is the next logical step: while still under the protective umbrella of a salary, slowly begin to amass new revenue generators. This does NOT mean to perform other "mini-jobs" for money, since that would be the same as working, but rather to create "investments" — this can be anything from investments in the stock market to getting books or mobile apps published that will continue bringing in money after you've "completed" them. The point is that you create/do something that brings in revenue while requiring as little maintenance as possible. Your first financial independence from your parents brought you financial freedom — "job-independence" will bring you the next freedoms: of living life at your own pace as an entrepreneur and choosing what to do with your time. You will still have to work plenty hard — even harder than before, but now that you will be working for

yourself, so you will feel much more motivated and passionate about it. It will be well worth it.

Additional Resources:
- *The 7 Habits of Highly Effective People: Powerful Lessons in Personal Change* by Stephen R. Covey
- *Losing My Virginity* Sir Richard Branson's autobiography
- *The 4-Hour Workweek* by Timothy Ferriss
- *The 4-Hour Body* by Timothy Ferriss

COMING OUT AS AN ATHEIST

You've watched the YouTube videos, you've read the atheism books such as *The God Delusion, God is not Great*, and watched many an episode of "The Atheist Experience." — Slowly, what once was dread and fear, transformed into a boiling new realization that you are now an atheist, and that your atheism is something to be proud of. However, it seems that many people around you, including your coworkers, friends and family may not have reached the same conclusion. The urge to tell everyone about your new beliefs is almost overwhelming, and it's becoming increasingly hard to hold back your opinions when occasionally religious topics come up. You also feel as if you are a dishonest lying hypocrite when you hold back your opinions, or even worse, if you are still pretending to be a believer. However, before you run around proclaiming to everyone that there is no God and that religion is silly and exists merely to tax the ignorant, you should ask yourself these simple questions:

1. Will doing so jeopardize your future?

For instance, you could be under the legal age, or your religious fundie parents could be supporting you through college or you could be living under their roof. While most parents might have to do some adjusting, if you live in a heavily religious part of town and your parents are of the devout kind, it would be very wise to avoid your urge to start preaching the gospel of Dawkins to them, and instead perhaps to act as an anthropologist — attend church if you must, ask plenty of questions, take notes. This way, you will be both informed about the Bible — more than you would as a theist, and you won't be kicked out of your house — which has actually happened to some. I've been given stories of people who were in effect disowned by their parents for coming out as an atheist. Luckily for me, when I told my mom, "Good news — I'm an atheist," all she said was "oh, you'll get over it." However — I'm in Eastern Europe, whereas the US "Bible Belt," Latin America, many Muslim nations and other spots will probably not be as open to this. Try to gauge the situation. You do not owe it to anyone to come out straight away if you think there is some risk.

On the other hand, you might very well decide you owe them enough respect not to volunteer to contradict their cherished beliefs. At least, become financially independent first, and move out, before confronting them with your change of views.

2. Will it affect your work?

I've told coworkers that I'm an atheist — they asked what the "*A*" pin I was wearing symbolized and I explained it to them. Indeed, at least one of my coworkers is an atheist. However, here in Eastern Europe it is not taken that seriously, and it would be like me saying that I support a different political party or football team — a mere curiosity but nothing to lose your job over. However, that might not be the case where you are. Atheism is knowledge — it will free you from all the baloney and guilt, but use it to your advantage, don't allow it to jeopardize your livelihood.

3. Will it affect your marriage/relationship?

Yes, yes, it will. Luckily for me, my girlfriend was an atheist, and things worked out so well that we got married. Of course, this is not her only quality, by far, and I love her dearly. I just want to emphasize the fact that having a long-term relationship with a partner with a differing religious view is not a good idea, especially if at least one of you takes their worldview seriously. I've read too many stories about distraught atheists — mostly males, losing their wives and kids due to arguments about religion and how to raise their kids. It creates a rift that is impossible to bridge without one party being forced to "shut up and live a lie."

If you are already in a relationship and have just deconverted, well, I am sorry, but chances are that it's not gonna work out if you try to convert the other person. Likewise, it creates an almost impossible situation for a couple when one member suddenly is "saved again" or converts to a strongly religious lifestyle.

4. Will it affect my friends?

It may. If they can't accept it, then find new friends.

Is it worth getting into debates with theists?

If your aim is to change minds you will be sorely disappointed. It is unlikely that after presenting some sound arguments and debunking the other side's misconceptions and logical fallacies the believer will say "gosh, you are right, I never thought about it — I guess God doesn't exist after all!" At best, you will make the believer doubt a little more than before, and deconversion might even occur if the believer is already "on the brink," that is, already has been pondering many of the ideas you are talking about and already full of doubt or unsure what to believe and looking for guidance. On the other hand, most people shy away from confronting such deeply-held beliefs, and resent having them cast into doubt.

That being said, deconversion is not the only reason to part take in a debate — for one, you can use it as an opportunity to test out your own assumptions and find your weak points. Just because you are an atheist doesn't mean that you are now automatically supposed to know all of the argufments, and realizing where you are deficient in said regard could be highly beneficial. There is nothing pertaining to shame in being out-debated by the believer, indeed, the key is to continue studying, reading new and informative books and to continue debating. For the new atheist this can prove highly therapeutic. I myself spent tens of hours debating theists, indeed mostly one in particular — we didn't change each other's minds and it seemed as if we "almost" convinced the other one, however this perception was quite illusory, on account of us feeling this at the same time, as though we both were winning. This could have been due to the fact that we shared so much information during our discussions that it was hard to understand why the other person's position had not yet shifted. He is still a good friend of mine and I think he is a good person, but I doubt he will ever change his mind.

You're a "Clergy Atheist"... Now What?

It's one thing to come out as an atheist to your family and friends, but what happens if you're not a mere "part of the flock" but the shepherd himself? This is much more common than you might think. A 2010 pilot study by Daniel C. Dennett and Linda LaScola documented the existence of such people: pastors, imams, rabbis, and other religious leaders who once were vehement believers but lost their faith over the years. It is really tough, if you think about it: your whole life is tied up in the community of worship. People who once admired you and asked you for advice would probably feel betrayed, or at the very least feel that, tragically, "you've lost your way." Furthermore, your entire livelihood is tied up in the church — most clergy do not possess other professional skills. Even if we include skills such as counseling, a clergyman will still have to be formally retrained as a counselor or psychologist prior to being able to work in that field — a feat that will require both time and effort.

The Richard Dawkins Foundation for Reason and Science created what is known as "The Clergy Project," which is reputed to have more than 556 members at the time of this writing. This online support group has extremely strict privacy guidelines, with anonymity and member screening prior to being able to join (to avoid people joining merely to "out" atheist clergy). Being an ordained religious leader and having to hide your true beliefs can be very damaging psychologically. You feel as if you are living a lie and "betraying" the people that look to you for guidance by not telling them the truth. Luckily, the Clergy Project community has people who have "traveled the road," so to speak, and can offer advice to newcomers on how to slowly distance themselves from their profession. The key seems to be to do it slowly: find another source of income or get some training/education in a non-religious profession, and then slowly become less and less active in the church and eventually resign. Some, like Teresa MacBain, who was a Methodist minister, took the more overt path by announcing her deconversion right on stage during an American Atheists convention.

ATHEISM AND MORALITY

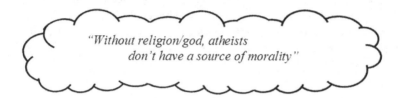

"Without religion/god, atheists don't have a source of morality"

After all of their other arguments fail, morality seems to be the last bastion of defense that many theists fall back to during debates. (See the section, "I would sin if there was no God.") However, even here, logically, they have no legs to stand on. Before we dive in further, let's get out our trusted dictionary[1] and get the word's definition, since this will help avoid confusion later on:

Morality
1. The quality of being in accord with standards of right or good conduct.
2. A system of ideas of right and wrong conduct: religious morality; Christian morality.
3. Virtuous conduct.
4. A rule or lesson in moral conduct.

Common ways people think of morality include:

- God-Given Absolute morality — Everything God says goes.
- Absolute/Objective morality — some "inherent" morality in the universe.
- Subjective morality — everyone has their own unique views on morality.
- Intersubjective morality — groups of people agree on sets of moral principles.

---

[1] http://www.thefreedictionary.com/morality

Why religious morality is inferior

The crux of religious moralities, and I have to underline the "s" since there is no such thing as single unified religious morality, is that there are as many religious moralities as there are religions, and even more if you count all the different views and "interpretations" of the believers. Each of those moralities claims to be THE morality, and would only get that THE-ness if the religion is itself the "true" one. If there indeed is some set of rules imbued in the universe, be it the Ten Commandments of Christianity, the Five Pillars of Islam, the Karmic laws of Buddhism, then those are by definition THE ultimate authority, and one better follow them or risk getting a bad afterlife, regardless of your personal opinions of those rules. Not following those rules and "creating your own" would be as mad as a citizen living by his own made-up laws in a society and being surprised if he gets arrested.

When looking at a set of religious moral principles from the outside, atheists and theists alike often forget this difference in perspective, and instead commence discussing the actual moral positions of the religion in question. The laws look very different when you think of them as "old texts passed down through tradition" rather than the absolute truth and the commands of the creator of the universe.

Believers often attempt to present the morality of their religion as the "superior one," regardless if you believe in their deities or not. This does not make much sense to me: if you actually read the Bible and not merely listen to apologists, you will notice that the vast portion of that morality lies in "serving/pleasing God," and all of humanity's well-being is somehow tied to that activity and to living a sin-free life — that is, a life which is in accordance with God's laws. These laws are "set in stone" and only subject to slight "reinterpretations." Secular morality, on the other hand, is all about increasing humanity's well-being and prosperity and decreasing suffering. It does not care about some imagined being, it is "by the people, for the people," and it changes and evolves naturally over time to reflect the changing values of society. Often, religions will try to claim the advances of secular morality as their own, when in reality they would have executed or mistreated you but a few hundred years ago for being a witch, adhering to "the wrong religion," not devout enough, or doing something socially unacceptable while ignoring such issues as slavery or cruelty to animals.

That's just the Old Testament

Let's have a look at some Christian morality:

> *When a man strikes his male or female slave with a rod so hard that the slave dies under his hand, he shall be punished. If, however, the slave survives for a day or two, he is not to be punished, since the slave is his own property.* (Exodus 21:20-21 NAB)

"But that's the Old Testament!" you might say — surely Jesus abolished slavery and said something to the effect of "thou shalt not own another human being?"

> *Slaves, obey your earthly masters with deep respect and fear. Serve them sincerely as you would serve Christ.* (Ephesians 6:5 NLT)

Oops.... Well this is awkward. Loads more where that came from — other religions have numerous examples of their own, perhaps enough for an entire new book. The point is not that religions don't have any good morality in them — they have plenty. The problem lies in that they have plenty of bad parts as well, and it takes our human judgment to distinguish them and "pick and choose" the good parts.

The "It doesn't matter because it was in the Old Testament" defense is easy to deal with as well. The Christian God is unchanging — how is it that his opinion of what's right and wrong changed? Could it be that his views "evolved" with the times? What blasphemy!

The Biblical Jesus was a staunch supporter of following the Old Testament:

> *"For truly, I say to you, till heaven and earth pass away, not an iota, not a dot, will pass the law until all is accomplished. Whoever then relaxes one of the least of these commandments and teaches men so, shall be called least in the kingdom of heaven; but he who does them and teaches them shall be called great in the kingdom of heaven."* (Matthew 5:18-19 RSV)
>
> *"It is easier for Heaven and Earth to pass away than for the smallest part of the letter of the law to become invalid."* (Luke 16:17 NAB)

And this is just a small scoop — there is a large list of quotes about not ignoring the Old Testament.[1] On the other hand, you can find verses seemingly proving that the Old Testament was abolished by Jesus — the Bible is a big book of multiple choice. Additionally, where are the Ten Commandments? In the Old Testament, that's where. It really matters how you examine these holy books — if you look at them merely as old texts which can be used to gain insight into the lifestyle, fear and dreams of ancient civilizations, then excellent, this is good stuff! If, on the other hand, you are looking at it as a guide on how to live your life and as the ultimate truth, well, here we have an issue. The reason that these books get criticized in ways shown above is that so many people to this day claim that they are their source of truth/morality.

If you do encounter the "well this is in the Old Testament so it doesn't count" defense — this is easily disproved as well, since Jesus himself told us many times not to ignore the Old Testament:

[1] http://www.evilbible.com/do_not_ignore_ot.htm

> *"For truly, I say to you, till heaven and earth pass away, not an iota, not a dot, will pass the law until all is accomplished. Whoever then relaxes one of the least of these commandments and teaches men so, shall be called least in the kingdom of heaven; but he who does them and teaches them shall be called great in the kingdom of heaven."*
> *(Matthew 5:18-19 RSV)*

There are many more phrases like this.

Biblical metaphor and citations out of context

Whenever someone brings up something to the effect of "well this is out of context," or "a metaphor," you can go the full route and proclaim "Well, I think God is metaphorical — it but represents the inner struggle of human beings and the struggle of society in general to overcome its limitations and live up to a higher standard." A defense that you might encounter is the "Well this is in the Old Testament so it doesn't count." There are no markings in any holy book that I'm aware of that denote which chapters/verses should and shouldn't be taken literally.

The "out of context" defense is easy to deal with. Open up the verse that was listed in the Bible — it should be easy even if you don't have an actual Bible nearby — just use Google, and look at the surrounding verses. Unless it says "the below verse is just a joke" (the Bible has no such labeling), you can be pretty sure that the verse was meant to be taken literally.

Excuses for troubling passages in scripture

Luckily, unlike the morality of religious texts, which is set in stone, so to speak, where the only possible way to make them less abominable was to "re-interpret" or downright ignore the inconvenient parts, the morality that *real* people use constantly evolves through the generations: things that were once not thought of as immoral, such as slavery, cruelty to animals, racism, child marriage, genocide are now despised, even though all of these things exist in Christian and Muslim, and other texts. Steven Pinker in *The Better Angels of Our Nature* describes how human morality has actually immensely improved over the past several thousand years, and how the world is actually a much safer and better place — it sounds unbelievable, but the illusion that "the world is getting worse and more violent" is simply due to the fact that we now have YouTube and television, and so are able to mourn shooting victims in another country minutes after said shooting happens. Since we are bombarded with various such news we naturally, and wrongly, assume that this means the world is becoming more violent, which it is not.

Apart from the previous problems with religious morality, all proponents of a God-based moral system run into the Euthyphro dilemma, which was created by Plato way before Christianity even existed. The premise is this:

> *Is something moral because God commanded it,*
> *or did God command it because it is moral?*

This distinction may seem unimportant at first glance, but it has devastating implications:

If something is moral because God commanded it, then such a moral system is necessarily subjective (it is God's subjective moral system), and hence is not absolute/objective.

If God commanded something simply due to it being moral, then God didn't create those morals, and is simply a messenger: as such, he would not be all-powerful since otherwise he'd create his own "absolute" morality, which would make it subjective, and create a headache for everyone involved.

Some apologists attempt to overcome this by claiming that "morality is in God's nature." However this merely moves the problem one step back: if it's "in his nature" then this would mean that he either designed his own nature and hence that he changed and is not eternal, or that it was already there — if so, who designed God's nature? If his "nature" is eternal does that mean he did not come up with his own views?

Additional Resources:
- Matt Dillahunty: The Superiority of Secular Morality (YouTube video)
- *The Better Angels of Our Nature* by Steven Pinker

SECULAR MORALITY

Most people today, apart from some extremists, actually adhere to a secular morality. Sure, it may have a varnish of religiosity somewhere, but if we were to still hold to the morality, of, say, Christianity we would still be owning slaves and stoning children for disobedience, as is shown here:

He that curseth his father, or his mother, shall surely be put to death. -- Exodus 21:17

The eye that mocketh at his father, and despiseth to obey his mother, the ravens of the valley shall pick it out, and the young eagles shall eat it. -- Proverbs 30:17

And another one, with bears:

And he went up from thence unto Bethel: and as he was going up by the way, there came forth little children out of the city, and mocked him, and said unto him, Go up, thou bald head; go up, thou bald head. And he turned back, and looked on them, and cursed them in the name of the LORD. And there came forth two she bears out of the wood, and tare forty and two children of them. -- 2 Kings 2:23-24

Since we do not kill children for heckling these days and consider slavery a despicable crime, now called "human trafficking" to make it sound even more illicit and lowly, today's followers of Christianity are obviously getting their morality elsewhere. That "elsewhere" is not a single source: rather it's what we, as a society, have attained through a slow and painful processes — from the struggle of the black community against racism and discrimination, to the strife of the LGBT activists in most parts of the world, the general consensus of what is and isn't socially acceptable is comparable to an ever-changing battleground of ideas rather than something that was written down once and is an "absolute truth."

Indeed, human beings are far from the only beings with morality — it is a pre-requisite for the many animals that live socially — including wolves, elephants and chimps. Wolves have a strong hierarchical structure so each member must know "his place" and what is and isn't acceptable. Elephants and chimps both mourn the dead — elephants have been known to visit "grave sites" of elephants and stand there for long periods of time, while chimp mothers can cling to dead babies for weeks before coming to grips with their loss. Apart from that, they all take care of those that they are close to and possess strong "in group" and "out group" differentiation ("he is part of us; it's OK if he is a jerk, we'll still take care of him — now those guys over there who are not in our group are EVIL and we shall smite them!") While we may pat ourselves on the back for being all sophisticated with our morality, we are far from the only species to possess it.

"The God of the Old Testament is arguably the most unpleasant character in all fiction: jealous and proud of it; a petty, unjust, unforgiving control-freak; a vindictive, bloodthirsty ethnic cleanser; a misogynistic, homophobic, racist, infanticidal, genocidal, filicidal, pestilential, megalomaniacal, sadomasochistic, capriciously malevolent bully."

— Richard Dawkins, The God Delusion

The morality we have today does not come from religion, no matter what anyone says. If it did, we'd actually be in a very sorry state. While the New Testament and Quran do contain passages about peaceful conduct, such as turn the other cheek, one actually has to strain to find them.

Matthew 11:20-30

Woe on Unrepentant Towns
Then Jesus began to denounce the towns in which most of his miracles had been performed, because they did not repent. 21 "Woe to you, Chorazin! Woe to you, Bethsaida! For if the miracles that were performed in you had been performed in Tyre and Sidon, they would have repented long ago in sackcloth and ashes. 22 But I tell you, it will be more bearable for Tyre and Sidon on the day of judgment than for you. 23 And you, Capernaum, will you be lifted to the heavens? No, you will go down to Hades. For if the miracles that were performed in you had been performed in Sodom, it would have remained to this day. 24 But I tell you that it will be more bearable for Sodom on the day of judgment than for you."

Matthew 10:34

King James Version (KJV)
Think not that I am come to send peace on earth: I came not to send peace, but a sword.

Quran (9:30) - "And the Jews say: Ezra is the son of Allah; and the Christians say: The Messiah is the son of Allah; these are the words of their mouths; they imitate the saying of those who disbelieved before; may Allah destroy them; how they are turned away!"

I do not wish to suggest that those books are "all-bad" — the point is that even devout believers use their own judgment to choose the good verses and ignore the bad ones. There are plenty of books out there identifying examples of "morality" from the different religions that we do not, in fact, find viable. In short, these books have plenty of interesting tidbits, including genocide of tribes that had the misfortune of being nearby and not being of the correct religion, as well as slavery, plagues, and ordinary cruelty. Furthermore, many of the victims of these salutary tales were then to continue suffering for all eternity in hell. How very nice. A good thing this is all fiction.

Atheist Morals

There are no tenets in atheism, for it is merely a lack of a belief in a deity. That being said, since it is now up to us as individuals to create our own morality, we can hold ourselves to a higher standard if we so choose. It is up to us to examine how we conduct our lives and make new choices: even if we choose to go on doing things the same way as before. It's our responsibility, now.

Vegetarianism as an example

There is no tenet in atheism that in any way condones or disapproves of vegetarianism, but we can take vegetarianism as an example. Steven Pinker, in his book *The Better Angels of Our Nature*, talks about the advancement of morality, and how humanity's "social circle" is ever-expanding, starting from the tribe, to the city, to the nation, to all humans, and now to animals.

One may also discuss the health and psychological benefits/disadvantages of being a vegetarian: while there is a correlation between longer a lifespan and vegetarianism, correlation by no means equals causation. For one thing, the demographic of westernized, relatively affluent people who are vegetarians usually includes more health-conscious individuals, less prone to smoking and alcohol; they might meditate; they probably have above-average access to healthcare. There is no conclusive evidence that "If you abstain from meat products, you will live X amount of years longer." If you do become a vegetarian, be sure to read the proper literature and eat properly and healthily.

I personally had a hard time giving up meat — and this was when I was a Buddhist. Nonetheless, the widespread adoption of vegetarianism may come with changing moral sensibilities (aided by rising meat prices).

Free Will

Many religious folks will claim that without the notion of the magical "soul" human beings are reduced to mere sacks of meat, to robots or automatons. In a rare show of support, many neuroscientists now posit that free will, and, in fact, to take it one step further, the notion of the "self," are all elaborate illusions created by our minds. Before going further, let's look up what "Free Will" actually is in a dictionary[1], since so many people have various notions about it:

Free Will

1.The ability or discretion to choose; free choice
2.The power of making free choices that are unconstrained by external circumstances or by an agency such as fate or divine will.

There are of course various definitions, but we'll stick to the above ones for the sake of consistency.

So what exactly makes the notion of "human beings as materialistic sacks of meat" so repugnant to the spiritualists out there? Religious folk somehow pre-suppose that if the soul were taken away, then free will would be too, and we would no longer have that magic which they like so much.

Suppose that we had all of the information from the start of the universe about the positions of every single atom/subatomic particle/etc., in the universe, and had an infinitely strong computer — we would be able to run

[1] http://www.thefreedictionary.com/free+will

a simulation and predict every single action that every human would ever do. This is determinism, and I think this seems reasonable (unless one dives into quantum mechanics, which I won't be doing here since I don't understand it).[1] In fact, scientists today are able to predict with some success what a person will choose before he consciously chooses it, by means of scanning that person's brain with complicated equipment.

The mere ability to predict an action does not diminish its free will aspect, however. And in fact, being unpredictable is usually not a good quality — if we had a "randomizer" inside our brains or in the "soul," which would make us behave unpredictably, that would not give us free will — it would merely make our actions incoherent. As such, I find that this notion of tying free will to unpredictability pointless. Indeed, the term "free will" has so much cultural baggage that I prefer to use a more neutral term — "self-determination."

For instance, if you tell me that tomorrow I will sleep, go to work, have lunch and possibly watch a TV show, as long as it's on a weekday, and this is at a time when I still haven't gotten filthy rich from this book and still have a job, you will be totally right. However, by your being able to predict that, you are not diminishing the value of my own choices to work where I want to work, eat what I want to eat and watch what I want to watch. To be sure, you could argue that I don't really have a choice, and that everybody must work — but this is not the case: there are countless people who don't work, out of their own choosing, and who don't watch TV shows, even though they have a TV.

While these discoveries destroy the poetic notions of the "magical free will" that is unpredictable and above science, and the notion that we are always conscious of how we make every decision, we are left with a more down to earth "self-determinism." If you are ever in a conversation with the believer and the topic of free will comes up, kindly ask them to define it, as it will avoid a lot of confusion.

Additional Resources:
- *How the Mind Works* by Steven Pinker
- *Phantoms in the Brain: Probing the Mysteries of the Human Mind* by V. S. Ramachandran
- *How We Decide* by Jonah Lehrer
- *Neurophilosophy: Toward a Unified Science of the Mind-Brain* by Patricia Smith Churchland

---

[1] "If you think you understand quantum mechanics, you don't understand quantum mechanics," — quote widely attributed to Richard Feynman.

RELATIONSHIPS AS AN ATHEIST

The old cliché "opposites attract" may be good for a romantic comedy film; however, when it comes to producing a stable long-term relationship, it is something to avoid. There is a reason why many faiths promote "marriage within the faith": it benefits the "religion" by creating a single stable family unit that will breed new adherents that will inherit that religion, and this type of single identity supposedly also makes the family unit more stable. However, it is not the religion that makes the relationship last longer; in fact recent studies have shown that evangelical Christians have the highest divorce rates in the US, and that the less "fundamentalist" the group is, the lower the divorce rates are. Atheists have some of the lowest divorce rates in the US, contrary to what many religious people would want to believe. This is mainly due to the way religion distorts people's ideas about sex, making them think it is "sinful" and that the only way to have non-sinful sex is to marry (and even then, many Christian denominations only consider sex non-sinful if it is for procreation). This leads a lot of highly religious Christians to marry early, in order to be able to have sex without sinning, and this leads to early divorces. Couples who marry (or indeed, begin "living together") later in life have a much higher satisfaction rate and far fewer divorces.

Back to my point — the more views that the partners have in common, the higher the chances that they will end up living together happily. The issues that tear many couples apart usually involve:

- Religion/Politics
- Kids (yes/no/how many?)
- Sexual preferences and frequency
- Lifestyle
- Money issues (who will work, who will take care of the kids, spending priorities, etc.)
- Marriage (yes/no/when?)

It may be tempting to overlook these during the first few months of a relationship, during the "honeymoon" phase; however, if you are looking for something long term it is vital find out about your prospective partner's views on these topics. I've heard far too many stories about families being broken apart when one member converts to a different religion or drops religious faith and becomes an atheist. Relationships can be hard to maintain anyway, and there is no need to make them even harder. Looking out for these "landmines" is key: for instance, religion may not seem important "now," but if you have kids, chances are that your religious partner will want to bring them up in their religion. Every situation is different of course, but it will still be a "competition" between you and your partner, either an overt emotional one or even a "friendly" one, regarding who will be the most successful in instilling their viewpoint. You may even decide that you are a non-argumentative type; but what will happen when your children will start fearing hell, or start spouting things that you know are absurd — as a parent, it will be your overwhelming instinct to correct them, and this may lead to conflict.

These days, with the invention of the Internet, finding like-minded individuals has become way easier — you are no longer bound to settle and be apologetic for your views, or to "compromise." You deserve someone who understands you and with whom you can feel comfortable. This is especially true if you have just recently deconverted and need someone for support to talk to and express your views freely — there is simply nothing more liberating than that. Of course, making a relationship and finding your "soul mate" (so to speak) is much more than merely being of the correct belief system: depending on gender, the advice may be different, but the point is you need to work on yourself and "get your act together." Read self-help books — I know this sounds cheesy, but as with all things in life, chances are you are not the first person with this problem — for every "unique" issue that you think you have, there have been millions of guys/girls with the exact same issue. I cannot overstate this enough — if you have a "problem area" in your life, do a quick Google search and you are bound to find numerous forum threads, blog posts and books — after that, it is your sacred duty to ingest all of that knowledge and use it to better yourself. If you want to change, the tools are all there, right at your fingertips.

ATHEIST PARENTING

How does the atheism aspect of your life relate to raising kids?
1.   Explore ancient "myths" and various world religions with your children.

Read to your child: read Greek mythology — of Zeus, Athena, etc.; teach your children about colorful figures like Thor and Loki (with the recent movies it shouldn't be too hard). Read about historical religions such as those of the Aztecs and ancient Egyptians. Explore a number of world religions such as Christianity, Islam, Judaism, Hinduism and Buddhism.

By reading all of these "stories" your child will become much less vulnerable to proselytizing and won't be as impressed when hearing about Christianity or the dominant religion of your region. It will be as if people walked up and started talking about Thor as if he were real, after you've just seen the movie. An added benefit is that your child will have learnt a lot of history and literature.
2.   Educate your children in critical thinking and the basics of "how we know things."

Whenever your child asks you about why something is the way it is, "I don't know — let's find out" is a perfectly valid answer. A great book to read with children is *The Magic of Reality*, where Richard Dawkins talks about the explanations various religions give for things such as "the birth of the universe" and "thunderstorms," and then gives the scientific side of the story.

This book is inherently beautiful both in its illustrations and textual content, and worth reading even if you don't have kids.

    3.   Explain the concept of indoctrination to your child.

It will only take 5 minutes (or 5 hours, if the conversation ignites), but you can explain the notion that when kids are young it is easy for adults to give them silly ideas; this is a concept every child should know. Use examples such as Santa Claus to illustrate your point.

    4.   Encourage your child's inquisitiveness and creativity.

While the constant badgering of "why is this__?" and "how does ___?" from younger children may seem annoying, but there is nothing worse than shutting down that questioning.

    5.   Love your child and let him/her choose!

The worst thing one can do, regardless of religious or political views, is to force your own views down the throats of your children. Even if your child becomes a monk or a republican, it is up to you to love your child and accept him for who he/she is.

Additional Resources:
- *Parenting Beyond Belief: On Raising Ethical, Caring Kids Without Religion* by Dale McGowan
- www.atheistparents.org
- *The Magic of Reality: How We Know What's Really True* by Richard Dawkins

---

THE IMPERFECTIONS AND QUIRKS OF YOUR MIND

I've named this chapter this way, specifically using the word "your," instead of something more amenable like "the imperfections of human minds" since that would allow you to sort of distance yourself from the impact of this chapter, as if all that will be described applies to "generic people" but not you, since you are of course perfect.

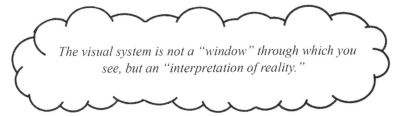

The visual system is not a "window" through which you see, but an "interpretation of reality."

If you are not too different from most people, you take it for granted that, if you were to look up from this book and look around, you would see a clear and precise representation of the "real" world — surely it is only mental patients that see things that are not there? Well, sort of...

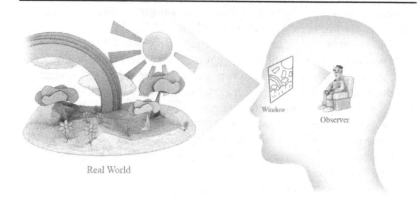

Above: The notion of the eye being the "window into reality" that provides a clear image of what is going on outside to you, the "observer."

For the most part of history, it was assumed that "what you see is what there is," however what, in reality is there? Please bear with me — I'm not claiming that there is no absolute reality, or anything like that — this book exists for me, just as it exists for you, and so do gravity and John McCain. The issue, rather, is in our varied perceptions: while the "eyes as the window into reality" notion sounds beautiful and simple, indeed it sounds obvious, I hereby assert that it is also misleading: if all you had was a "window," a camera, if you will, to view reality, all you'd get is tons of useless raw data. Human eye cones contain red, green and blue receptors (this is why computer monitors and televisions use these colors to create images). If, however, all you have is raw data from an eye or webcam, you will get something pretty much useless:

R=234 G= 23 B= 32	R=234 G= 23 B= 32	R=134 G= 23 B= 32	R=132 G= 23 B= 32	R=233 G= 23 B= 32
R=234 G= 12 B= 32	R=233 G= 23 B= 31	R=200 G= 21 B= 34	R=234 G= 22 B= 34	R=236 G= 21 B= 32
R=234 G= 23 B= 32	R=234 G= 23 B= 31	R=233 G= 23 B= 32	R=236 G= 23 B= 32	R=234 G= 23 B= 32
R=234 G= 21 B= 33	R=234 G= 23 B= 41	R=234 G= 23 B= 12	R=234 G= 23 B= 12	R=234 G= 23 B=10

SCARY RAW MEANINGLESS DATA!!

What am I supposed to do with that??

(Where R means Red, B means Blue, and G means Green)

What's more, this is just a tiny 4 by 5 grid, whereas a High Definition monitor contains 1920x1080 pixels (pixels are just a fancy way of saying dots that have varying amounts of Red, Green and Blue in them), and the human eye contains immensely more — with estimates ranging from 105 to 576 megapixels. The wild difference in the estimates occurs because the human eye doesn't have the same density of these receptors everywhere, but rather more in the middle and less and less towards the sides, this is why your "peripheral vision" is always a bit more blurry. However, fear not: your brain is always doing a wonderful job of preventing you from noticing or caring.

So back to my point — if all you had were these values popping up in front of you, you'd be blind as a bat (bats aren't blind but it sounds nice). Instead, what the brain does is it transforms all of this weird random information into something you can use. However, don't be fooled into thinking that it merely allows you to see colors instead — if all you had was access to "the colors," you'd still be effectively blind, since without your visual system telling you what things are, it would be as if you were staring at abstract paintings, which are full of interesting shapes and squiggles, and a variety of colors, but no meaning:

It is only after this "raw data" goes through your visual cortex that you realize that the large dark tall thingy in front of you is a tree, and that the round bright thingy is the sun. Furthermore, all of this analysis happens "under the hood" and you just get the results: if you look at a building, you instantly know it's a building, you do not need to ask yourself questions about the shape and composition of the building, unless of course you land on an alien planet where buildings are star-shaped and float inside large circles. Indeed, if you do insist that you do such thinking, and that you know that a building is a building because hey, it has this cubic shape, has rectangular doors with 4 corners, windows that are also rectangular and reflective, and so forth, I'd tell you that you were wrong, since if you did this mental exercise for every object that you see, you'd either go insane or go throw away this book. Rather, while you can of course justify why you think something is a building and something is a turnip, those justifications happen after you've already pre-determined what it was; these are separate tasks, which is exactly what I'll talk about in this chapter.

When it comes to things like whether or not that black circle on the ground is an open manhole, a painted-on black circle, or an oil slick, the behind-the-scenes decision-making may be akin to the UN security council, with various parts vying for "their" version of events, and other parts overruling them — it is only after the final decision has been made that we get the result. Of course, the result is not always correct: think of looking at optical illusions that trick our "eyes" while the logical parts of our brains clearly tell us what's going on.

With the brain, the best way to find out about what it does and how it does it is by observing patients with damage to specific localized regions of their brains. This allows us to deduce that it was that region that did the function that the person is now unable to do: there are, for example, people who are unable to distinguish or recognize faces: they see all of the separate features such as lips, ears and eyes, but are unable to "put it all together" to form a semblance of a face, and hence can't recognize even their loved ones, except through clues such as clothes, scars and tattoos.

Interestingly, when inside a MRI (Magnetic Resonance Imager), the same part of the brain which is used for distinguishing faces lights up for people who are car enthusiasts when they are shown pictures of cars.

With "Apperceptive visual agnosia," patients are not able to tell different visual shapes apart, recognize or copy them. Patients with a slightly different condition are merely unable to copy them.

People with "Associative visual agnosia," on the other hand, will be able to tell you that the round orange thing in front of them is used to play sports, and is bouncy, but will fail at telling you that it is a basketball.

People with "Cerebral achromatopsia" will be able to see colors, but will have difficulty in categorizing colors or telling them apart. They are not color-blind, mind you, but some mechanism that makes it easy for us to group school buses and bananas is somehow not working properly for them.

Look at your hand and locate your thumb and pinky finger. I said look, don't keep reading, I'll wait a bit...

It was easy, I assume; however, people with Finger agnosia would not be able to accomplish this — apparently, there is an entire system in the brain devoted to being able to distinguish fingers!

Look around you and name some of the objects that you see: it was easy and automatic, and you never broke a sweat. People with "Form agnosia" can, however, perceive only details and parts of objects, but not them in their entirety.

You are presumably able to read this text fairly easily. However, people who have undamaged eyes but who suffer from "Pure alexia" are unable to recognize text — it appears to them like a text which was written in a foreign alphabet.

I could go on listing these till supper, but the point is this: without dedicated machinery which does all of the heavy lifting for you and just gives you the results to work with, you would not be able to "see" the world in any meaningful way. Indeed, people who have been blind since birth or from a young age have to learn/re-learn to see after regaining their vision, which can take weeks or months, in some cases.

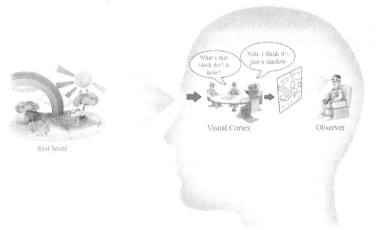

The "UN-Council" of Vision [1]

In the next section, I'll argue that just as we have automated machinery that gives us the result of what we saw, we have just such equipment that tells us what we think and decide.

What does the above information about how people see have to do with this book? Everyone, including you, my good reader, operates under the assumption that the thoughts that come into your head are arrived at through rational internal decision-making. Indeed, economists base their "science" on the notion that human beings are rational decision makers whose aim it is to maximize their own benefit and which they'll do through

[1] Note: the visual cortex is actually in the back of the head.

thought-out means. And, while there are instances of human beings acting rationally, most of the time we use mental shortcuts, because humans are, well... lazy.

Laziness, you see, is not the bad thing it is always made out to be, otherwise all of the lazy folk would have been weeded out through evolution — indeed another way of phrasing "laziness" is being economical and conserving energy.

Because our brains are still the brains that our ancestors used 50,000 years ago, they did not have time to adapt to such an ecosystem as we have today, with price lists, statistical probabilities, decimals, profit margins and the like: we evolved for an environment that was logically far simpler, where the tasks of the day involved finding a suitable mate, not stirring resentment by your group, and, if you perchance saw three lions enter a cave and only two exit shortly thereafter, deciding whether or not it was safe to enter said cave. We developed certain shortcuts and rules of thumb that, while not always accurate, served us well overall without requiring us to think very much. It is a pity that these same shortcuts sometimes cause us trouble when applied in the current world.

Just as there are optical illusions, there are also logical illusions: You have a baseball bat and ball, together they cost $1.10, and the bat costs $1 more than the ball. How much does the ball cost? If you are like most people, you answered that the ball costs 10 cents. That is the intuitive answer that "pops out." However, this answer is also wrong — the correct answer is that the bat costs $1.05 and the ball costs $0.05 (this is a really old problem, hence the cheap prices). Don't feel bad, most students from high-end universities such as MIT or Harvard answer the same way.

In *Thinking Fast and Slow*, Daniel Kahneman argues that there are two distinct and separate systems in the brain for solving logical conundrums and decision-making (and here, to be very clear, he doesn't imply that they are located somewhere specific in the brain, but rather, that these are the two ways our brains can solve problems). The first one is the one you used above, which is the "fast" system, which gives you quick and efficient judgments that are "mostly right," but which can be fooled, and the "slow" system, where you actually consciously go through a task, slowly and deliberately thinking through all of the steps.

Have you ever been in a situation where a solution to a problem you were thinking about "jumps out at you?" Indeed, this phrase is so familiar that surely you have, and the mere asking you of that question prompted you to reach into memory, and, paradoxically, the memory of some problem being solved by the solution jumping out at you itself "jumped out" at you. Yet, still we assume that it is "us," as in the conscious self, which solved the problem. Did we really do that (manually compute everything), or were we just given the results from somewhere deep inside our minds, a place which we cannot consciously access? If I were to ask you to think of a king with a crown, with a large beard, sitting on a throne in a large room, you would instantly "receive" said imagery. But how did you get it? Did you manually go dig through your memories, comparing all of them, and struggling to distinguish between a picture of a green mini-van and one of a king with a crown? Some efficient system that you take for granted did it for you.

It is only thanks to this "received guidance from the innards of your mind" that you are able to function at all: In *Descartes' Error: Emotion, Reason and the Human Brain*, Antonio Damasio talks about his patient "Elliot," who, after undergoing some frontal lobe surgery, appeared quite normal. However, he soon noticed that something was very, very wrong: he lacked all motivation and felt as though he were an "uninvolved spectator" when talking about his life, and there was no detectable emotion. His wife, whom he was happily in love with prior to the tumor-removing surgery, soon left him, and he lost his job and was unable to gain a new one. He was also unable to get any sort of government assistance, since, as far as anyone could see, there was nothing wrong with him. However, when talking to him, you soon get very frustrated: small decisions, such as when to set up the next appointment, which would take a "normal" person a rather small amount of time, seemed to take ages — indeed, you could tear out your hair over the course of several hours listening to all the pros and cons of having the next appointment for every hour of every day of the next week, all dispassionately and logically thought through but with no hint of a decision in sight. The fact that we do not possess the power of computers makes it painfully slow to come to any decision without involving emotion. It is only by feeling something — that tinge of approval, that we decide "Hey, that can of peas looks like what I'm looking for." Indeed, for most of human history emotion was considered this thing that clouds judgment, and that which all reasonable men should strive to get rid of, when it is the sole thing that allows us to function. Emotions are not just random impulses that sway us into unreason — sure, some do, and it is always best to be in control of your emotions and not to get too passionate; however that is still vastly different from not having any at all: emotions and the mind may be compared to a boat with oars. If you are not in control of your emotions, then the oars move haphazardly and the boat doesn't really go anywhere, it is only if you are calm and in control, that you can use your emotions (the oars) to reach your desired goal. However, having no emotions would be like not having oars — you would also not get anywhere.

Indeed, emotions, it is argued, are not just responses to stimuli to be ignored, but the results of calculations, albeit sometimes imperfect ones. From an evolutionary standpoint this makes perfect sense — a gazelle would have no use for text with commands printed in front of its eyes if it can't read, so the information it receives should be in easy to understand, emotional form:

- Lion –> emotion of danger, fear (queue to run away).
- Meadow with grass –> impulse to eat, but some caution and fear as well — better look around first.

While no one would argue with the above examples, the below, to which I have been leading up to, are both obvious and disconcerting at the same time:

- Posters for several movies in the cinema –> you get a feeling that "Hey, THAT one is the one I like."

- You are searching for a job, you see several job offerings –> "That one doesn't seem that nice, but THIS one seems like a decent occupation."

So, you would say, so what? You would be able to provide me with reasons as to why THAT job in particular is the one you want, or why this movie is the one you want to see, but the fact is that when you were actually choosing, you didn't think those thoughts, you just "decided" — and how did you do that? Well, it sort of "came to you." Hence my point. It is only when you consciously problem solve, as you do when learning a new skill, figuring out a math problem, or finding out why that bit of computer code isn't working or why the car won't start, that you are actually coming up with a decision consciously.

But if our brains pre-decide our actions for us, of what use is "consciousness"?

Reading all of this, you might begin to wonder what the actual role of consciousness, your "essence," or free will, if you prefer, really is. Instead of doing all of the work ourselves, it's as though some weird machinery that is part of us yet which we do not have conscious access to does all of the work for us. It may surprise you then, that such notions as "consciousness" and "free will" are historically quite recent phenomena, and only date back several thousand years. In *The Origin of Consciousness in the Breakdown of the Bicameral Mind*, Julian Jaynes argues that up until very recently, we did even less "thinking" and "being conscious" than we do today: for evidence of that, we can just open up any piece of literature that is several thousand years old — be it the Old Testament, *The Iliad*, or *The Epic of Gilgamesh* — when reading such texts, what struck me the most was that I had real difficulty identifying with the characters in those myths — and not just from a moral or cultural background: they sort of seemed "fake," without any real thought behind their actions, doing but not reminiscing, not considering possibilities, and the like — just "doing." There was no depth to them that we see in even the most badly written books or movies of today: they seem, while experiencing human emotions, to also completely "lack" some essential parts, and seem primitive and brutish. When some type of moral contention or decision-making does arise, it is usually in the form of a deity that "speaks" to the hero, and when the hero mentions this fact to others, he is not regarded as crazy and what he says is taken at face value.

Of course, one could simply say that back then people simply didn't know how to write as well as we do now, and that all of these conversations with gods are mere poetic devices, but Julian Jaynes argues that, instead of viewing those events through the filters imposed upon us by the modern world, maybe we should take them more at face value — after all, when Joan of Arc said that she heard God speak to her and therefore wouldn't repent to save her life, was she being "poetic"? — It seems disrespectful to even suggest such a thing. Indeed, we take it for granted that today everyone is literate, has at least a basic education and has at least a vague understanding that thinking occurs in the brain. However, up until very recently literacy was extremely low, usually in single digits. Common sense notions that we take for granted today were not so clear back then — such as the fact that if you hear a stray thought in your head, it is just you thinking and not "demons."

Imagine such a person hears a stray thought — he has no idea it's just inside his head. In today's society we would think no more of it, but there it was allowed to develop, and through constant reaffirmation the person would eventually not just hear thoughts as a normal person does, but back then it could easily reach such a state that is today reserved only for mental patients which really do hear voices. Jaynes argues that this was much more widespread in antiquity, and instead of having a pinch of emotion here and there to gently guide us, we often times heard real god-like voices that told us what to do and ordered us around. — It is only later, with the propagation of literacy, that instead of hallucinating voices we started writing commandments down, and the "potency" of these voices disappeared since writing is easier to ignore than that blaring voice in your head. Hence the gods became absentee gods that required praying to, instead of directly showing up and telling you what to do. Prior to that, everyone it seems, according to Jaynes, had voices in their heads, that they attributed to a god of some sort, which was in fact their right hemisphere telling them what to do. However, I'd take it with a grain of salt: Richard Dawkins wrote, regarding this book:

> It is one of those books that is either complete rubbish or a work of consummate genius, nothing in between! Probably the former, but I'm hedging my bets.

I recommend reading that book for yourself, but regardless, we can safely conclude that the human brain is a complex tool, a device, if you will, that does its best to give you useful information, answers to questions and the like; however, it can also be wrong at times. The biggest issue about it is that (unlike a computer program that may tell you when it's malfunctioning), the human brain has no "error messages," and so we are often misled into thinking that our decisions are well thought-out and that we have a clear understanding of reality, when in fact we could be far off the mark. Mental patients are the extreme example of this case, but everyone's brain has in-built shortcuts, optimizations and faults, that we ought to at least be aware of. The next chapter will focus on exactly that.

Additional Resources:
- *How the Mind Works* By Steven Pinker
- *Phantoms in the Brain: Probing the Mysteries of the Human Mind* by V. S. Ramachandran
- *The Origin of Consciousness in the Breakdown of the Bicameral Mind* by Julian Jaynes

Human Cognitive Biases

Humans are wired with "mental shortcuts" which allow us to make decisions "on the fly" without hours and hours of deliberation. A side effect of this is that while "efficient," these shortcuts do not always produce the most correct results.

One cannot talk about cognitive biases without talking about Daniel Kahneman and Amos Tversky, who, with their efforts which later resulted in a Nobel Prize, were able to establish a cognitive biases list which documented the ways in which humans commonly make incorrect decisions and logical mistakes. What you will see below is far from an exhaustive list, but I find these to be the most fun and entertaining ones.

Confirmation bias

We love a strong and coherent worldview, enjoy knowing that "we are right," and search out information that supports our views, however often, without realizing it, we also quietly ignore information that we do not agree with, or lessen its weight.

For example:

> A believer is searching for his keys. After an hour of searching to no avail he prays, and almost instantly is able to find said keys — this strengthens the believer's faith even more.

The actual reason, be it luck, or the fact that he stopped for a second and calmed down to pray, is irrelevant — rather what matters is that we collect all of those "little things" that support our views into the giant amalgamations that are our beliefs. Only if there is overwhelming evidence to the contrary, and sometimes not even then, does a belief change occur.

News channels are another great example: we prefer to surround ourselves with information with which we agree, rather than with information which we think is biased, faulty, or downright stupid. This all makes sense, and we all do it automatically, however the downside to this strategy is that we create an "information bubble" where we only surround ourselves with YouTube videos, news channels, friends, and books that we do not find objectionable or even challenging, and as such, our opinions get cemented. In this case, an antidote would be to read a book which contradicts your worldview every once in a while — it may feel horrible, grating even, to read a lot of such material — you may feel as though you are wasting your time when you could be absorbing "real" information, but it's worth it, and key to an open mind. I for instance have read The Bible, The Holy Quran, The Book of Mormon, among others, and while it did seem grueling at times, I do not regret the experience and think I am better off for it. Does this mean you should spend hours watching Fox News? No.

Availability bias

The world is a dangerous place — imagine you are sitting in an airplane that is about to take off, and, assuming you are not a frequent flier, chances are that you will inevitably think of a movie where a plane crashes or has some sort of malfunction — even if you are not afraid per se, your mind might still bring such a scenario up while you are waiting for half an hour on the runway or having your long flight. Indeed, there are things in this world that we hear about often on the news, such as shark attacks, terrorism, being killed in an armed robbery, or perhaps an earthquake or hurricane, which we assume are the things "to watch out for."

However, people are usually killed by much more mundane things which surround them on a day-to-day basis — all of the above are statistical flukes when compared to the "real" things you should be scared of: dying of a heart attack, old age, cigarette use related illnesses, and car accidents. Indeed, shark attacks usually kill less than 10 people during an entire year, while dying from smoking too much causes roughly half a million deaths in the US every year, and the amount of people that die from automobile accidents is vastly greater than the amount of people that die in wars.

The reason that we first assume that more deaths are caused by those "exciting" events that I first listed, is that when people are asked to imagine causes of death, or anything else for that matter, they go digging into their heads for examples, and where do you get them from? If you've had a relative die in a car accident or from smoking then you are probably well aware of the risks and it instantly jumped out at you, however mostly people get their information from the mass media, be it YouTube or the 24-hour cable news. And of course, the news will not bore you every day with statistics of how people are still dying from smoking, with breaking news reports from hospital wards, nor are they interested in constantly informing you about how old people are constantly dying from old age. Sure, don't get me wrong, those things are *sometimes* mentioned, sometimes the reports are even very good, but the point is that that is not the "meat" of the news: it is not attention grabbing. News needs to sell, and what sells better — a young girl who bravely fought off a shark and has something inspirational to say about becoming a wildlife researcher when she grows up, or some old people, wasting away from diabetes in an old folk's home?

Hence the imbalance — when we try to think of examples, be it of "ways to die" or anything else for that matter, we will automatically make the mistake of thinking that if we have an easier time remembering some things, then surely those must be common. This worked very well before the invention of television or books, when people lived in villages or hunter-gatherer groups, recounting stories of their exploits. In the modern world though, some extra thinking is naturally required.

Anchoring

The anchoring effect is why products which are marked "50%" off suddenly seem more attractive,[1] or why used car dealerships first post a ludicrous price on their cars, which allows you to get a "great deal" after some bargaining.

The focusing effect

The focusing effect is when you get fooled into judging a large proposition —buying a car or house, by focusing on one of the smaller details — for example the bright red paint. Okay, that one was obvious, but this issue tends to occur when the question is more open-ended.

In *Thinking, Fast and Slow*, Daniel Kahneman asked a simple yet devious question: "Who do you think is happier — Californians or Midwesterners?"

Chances are you surmised that living in California must make you happier than in an average city. Here you are not alone: both Californians and commoners alike responded in exactly the same way when asked about who they thought was happier — they naturally assumed that it was the Californians that were happier. However, both were wrong: when it comes to actually rating happiness, the two were not really distinguishable. Why does this happen? We forget that apart from the initial image of California, there are also day-to-day issues to deal with, like traffic jams, going to work, bills to pay, kids to feed, probation hearings to attend, and so forth — and people live real lives, not "snapshot lives" where they spend their entire days walking around the fresh-looking mountains and visiting the Golden Gate Bridge (that would be the tourists). When you were first provided with this question, I can assume your brain didn't bring up the work/kids/probation hearings imagery (unless of course you live in California) and just used what was given: better climate and scenery = more happiness.

Furthermore, we tend to lose sight of the fact that novelty wears off. If you were to move to San Francisco, California, I'm sure you would be ecstatic for the first few weeks and even months, and you might of course love the city for the rest of your life. However, humans adapt, and after that "honeymoon period" wears off, you will be left with a more quiescent appreciation of the city, combined with a much better understanding of what it means to actually live there.

Do you think that amputees and blind people are as happy as we are? Do you think YOU would be as satisfied with your life if you were to lose a leg? Chances are, you'd say no: life would be much more difficult, you wouldn't be as physically appealing, you wouldn't be able to do all of fun sports that you used to do. When asked this question, most people answer with a resounding "no," and newbie amputees and the newly blind answer

---

[1] Nowhere is it guaranteed that the same item was previously priced at twice as much.

in the same way. However, people who have been amputees for a while and for whom the novelty has worn off, as well as people who know long-time amputees and blind people, answer that "yes, you will be just as happy."

Why does this occur? When you think of losing a leg or a set of eyes, you think of how that would feel, of all of the things you'll lose. However, just as in the previous example, you will fail to appreciate that after a while you'll get used to it and return to your median level of happiness — the "novelty" and shock of the change will wear off. You will still have things to do: for instance, if you become blind, it might mean that instead of going to a tedious job every day, you can spend your days listening to audiobooks while drinking a nice warm coffee and with a cat on your lap. Doesn't seem that bad, now, right?

We still have difficulty with this, since when we imagine any change, be it becoming president or amputee, we think of it like this:

> The way we are right now + the change.

However, this is the short-term view; after a while it becomes:

> The way we are right now + the change + lots of things that happened afterwards to deal with the change + even more unexpected things.

Of course, it is impossible to predict or even be aware of these things most of the time, so our brain does the easy thing and goes with the first way. This is why we greatly overestimate the long-term impact of events such as winning the lottery, divorce, death in the family, moving to a new state, and so on, on our emotional well-being.

The "availability cascade"

The "availability cascade" is known by other names but the essence is, "Repeat something long enough and it will become true." This is why propaganda and advertising works. It is why people now think the US is a Christian nation, and that Creationism deserves an "equal amount of time" to be discussed in public classrooms. It can, of course, also be used to your advantage and to the advantage of humankind: messages about wildlife preservation, healthy living, critical thinking, and so forth, may also be spread in such a fashion. But this cognitive bias makes no differentiation between the real and unreal — for that, some actual thinking would be required.

The "bias blind spot"

This is an inception-style cognitive bias where we fail to appreciate that we ourselves have biases or can make decisions which are biased, as if by reading about these biases, we somehow become "exempt" from them. It helps to come to terms with the fact that we are prone to cognitive biases, and as such the best we can do is attempt to notice them and give in to them a bit less often. Denial, however, is not the solution.

Choice-supportive bias

Better known as "backwards rationalization," choice-supportive bias is when we think back to the decisions we made, and our mind downplays any negative aspects of that decision and instead creates an inner story, an inner narrative if you will, showing why the choice we made was the best possible choice under the circumstances.

> "Actually, I'm really glad I got that car — it's economical and low maintenance."

> "I'm really glad I moved to Alaska, even though it's cold. The money and the company are great, and I do love all of the scenery."

> "Going to prison isn't so bad — in fact, it builds character."

The endowment effect

Owning something makes you value it more. An item, if you were in possession of it for at least some period of time, is valued more by you than items of a similar quality which you never owned. Some people have attempted to explain this with the notion that you build memories of experiences while owning that item, and, while I could understand why that occurs with, say, a car or a motorcycle helmet, I still fail to understand why I hold onto old video cards and other computer innards that I will most likely never use but still keep "just in case," rather than selling them, since their value is diminishing as the years go by and now they are probably worth very little indeed.

The IKEA effect

This effect is a close cousin of "The Endowment Effect," only here, in addition to valuing something more merely due to owning it, you value something even more if you created it. This is why IKEA furniture is so popular: not only does it cost less by cutting out the paid assembly worker and giving that role to the consumer, it also costs less to transport since it is shipped in flat boxes. An additional surprising benefit is that having built the furniture themselves, the consumers were more satisfied with it. They have memories of how they built it and the effort they put into it, and hence are more fond of it. This applies to anything you create, be it a vase you made in pottery class, a painting, or even this book that I'm right now writing which I think will be the most amazing thing ever — certainly better than similar books.

The bandwagon effect

It is much easier to "go with the group" instead of being the unpopular one and feeling like an outcast because you think their ideas don't make sense. Indeed, straight from our evolutionary past, the most successful individuals were those that were able to organize themselves into close-knit groups with a common purpose, and naysayers and skeptics were not really appreciated since they could lower the overall morale and "purpose" of the group. In today's world, this can be disastrous, with groups being filled with "yes men" that are afraid of challenging the status quo since that might mean they will lose their popularity and support. In actuality, though, while it is easier said than done, it is best to strive to point out nonsense whenever you find it — be it to your boss, romantic partner or group of friends — people that can appreciate quality in you are much rarer than people who would merely see this as an affront, but if you find your niche, you will be greatly valued.

Consistency bias

Our inner narrative craves consistency. We like to think that we are more or less the same people that we always were, perhaps with more self-control, wisdom and experience.

Indeed, we need to have this "narrative of self" so much that our brains deceive us into thinking we were more similar in the "olden times" to the way we are now than we actually were. We think that our views on drugs, on smoking, on sex, on politics and religion were always not too distant to what we currently think. However, actually testing this by asking students their views, and then asking them again of what their views were once some years have passed reveals that the answers given for "views when they were younger" more closely resemble the views that they hold now, rather than the views they used to hold.

Indeed, children only gain the ability to understand and remember that they used to not know things or hold different opinions after a certain age: prior to that, if you were to tell a child an interesting fact, or reveal some information to them, and ask if they knew this before, for example yesterday, you'd get a "yes." The child is not yet able to imagine his previous state of not knowing or of knowing something different which has now been corrected. It seems, even grownups still retain some remnants of this, although of course to nowhere near such a dramatic degree.

The cross-race effect

People who are not often in contact with or do not often see peoples of another race will initially have more difficulty identifying peoples of other races. Also known as "they all look alike to me" effect. This is now much less common, especially in multi-cultural countries such as the US and the

United Kingdom, as well as due to the advent of television. This should not be confused with racism, where the inferiority of a race is implied. Indeed, I had a chance to experience this when I returned from Indonesia, where I studied in a school full of Indonesians, Indians and Chinese, into a school of people that were all white. For a short while, I had trouble telling my new white classmates apart (I'm also white): their haircuts, facial features and the like were all so similar! After a while, though, this effect wore off. I believe that the links to racism are only valid if you intentionally don't want to have anything to do with said race, or intentionally don't want to intermingle or recognize them.

The "Google effect"

Google and the Internet have made us all lazy: the incentive to remember is diminishing greatly, since instead of wasting all of that valuable brainpower bothering to remember the capital of Estonia, you will be tempted to "just Google it." There have been outcries that Google and the Internet are making us dumber. However, this is unfair.

There is an ancient Egyptian dialogue between one of the gods — one, who among other things, created writing, and the pharaoh. The pharaoh criticizes the god since people will no longer need to use their minds, and as such will become forgetful since everything will just be written down and there will be no need for memorization.[1]

In traditional societies different members of the group are unconsciously tasked with remembering different things (Indeed, this is easily seen today with the notion of specialties and professions). Also, even in a husband-wife relationship, it is not uncommon for the wife to be the one who "remembers the name of that one aunt" while the husband remembers the route to that good restaurant. Indeed, it is the fundamental division of labor. It's just that we started incorporating the Internet into this "group" that was once only people. So as such, there is really nothing "bad" about this phenomenon. If you want to actually become proficient at something, mere Googling won't suffice (though it will be a great start) — you will have to actually practice.

Hindsight bias

After some event has transpired you "knew all along" that it was going to turn out that way. "You knew that the stock market was going to crash" yet still invested, you "knew that you shouldn't have driven drunk" yet drove and got arrested. You "knew" Obama was going to win the election. This "wisdom," however, appears only after the fact. Prior to that, you may have suspected, hoped or dreaded, but there was much less certainty.

---

[1] To top matters off, the entire dialogue was actually created by Plato http://en.wikipedia.org/wiki/Phaedrus_%28dialogue%29

Additional Resources:
- *Thinking, Fast and Slow* by Daniel Kahneman and Amos Tversky
- *Predictably Irrational, Revised and Expanded Edition: The Hidden Forces That Shape Our Decisions* by Dan Ariely

IS IT WORTH ARGUING WITH THEISTS?

Having read all of the arguments for and against the existence of god(s), and having listened to numerous debates, it is easy to start feeling like Neo from *The Matrix* (1999), where you have all the counter arguments and can identify all of the logical fallacies. Alas, reality tends to differ: indeed, many a person has compared arguing with theists to "playing chess with a pigeon" — it doesn't matter that you know all of the "rules" of proper discourse if the pigeon is simply going to knock all of the pieces over and cover everything with bird dung.

It really depends on what you are trying to accomplish in said "debate." Here are some possible outcomes:
1. Gain a deeper understanding and respect of each other's belief system, or at least the "appearance of."
2. Both parties "agree to disagree."
3. One or both of the parties gets upset/angry/etc.
4. One of the parties changes their belief system (unlikely), or at least has it shift a bit.
5. You can practice debating skills but there won't be any real change of beliefs on either side.
6. You will feel better/freed.
7. Other people will learn something from the debate.

Pick your battles — especially if you are not self-sufficient and the person you will be debating has influence over your life and has strong religious views.

There have been many a story of religious parents kicking out their kids after finding out they were atheists. There have been stories of people losing their jobs as well. On the other hand, in other communities this hardly has any impact whatsoever.

You will be unlikely to convince the other party of your views through debate, and indeed, when will you stop? Will you take it upon yourself to convince the entire world? While this worthwhile goal will be great for the atheist community, this type of "evangelism," that borders on fanatical, always makes me a bit queasy since that's "just what religions do" — then again, I wrote this book.

Indeed, "feeling better," as if "confessing your sins" or "having a burden lifted" is possibly the premier reason why one starts telling people, especially in a conservative community, about their beliefs. It was my experience after getting my newfound worldview that I was living a "lie," and that the way people perceived me was different from who I really was. This made me feel dishonest so I soon started telling people, till it was no longer a big deal. It depends on your environment.

After outing yourself as an atheist, if you are from a religious community, you might lose friends, acquaintances, and even family members. This was not my experience, but many a person from other parts of the world have been less fortunate — you should, of course, take all of that into account prior to "outing yourself." However, if someone wishes to no longer to be your friend because of your newfound beliefs or asks you to stop expressing your opinions, are they really your friend? If someone converted from one religion to another, chances are his choice would be more or less respected. Why should atheistic beliefs be respected less, considering all of the actual thinking, reading and bravery you had to undergo to acquire them?

In *A Manual for Creating Atheists*, Peter Boghossian argues that this type of discourse should not take on the form of a "debate," and speaks of techniques used in correctional institutions and psychotherapy. Whether or not religiosity is a mental disorder is a good question: if only a minority of people were religious, then I would bet all my money that they would be considered delusional and referred to psychiatrists. However, this was exactly what was practiced at various periods by the Soviet Union, which also did the same for dissenting political opinions — we should, therefore, be very careful in how we label religion. Most human beings have a natural propensity towards religiosity, and as such we enter this grey area.

PARALOGIC COMPLIANCE AND RATIONALIZATION
Or, why religious logic still works on people

All of us have vague ideas about hypnosis. Once, a class of psychology students was told that their right arms could not move under hypnosis — something that up to this point had never been observed. However, when under hypnosis the students were asked to move their right arms, they could not.

It's not that the students were hypnotized into believing that they couldn't move them — there was no such mention during the hypnosis session itself. Rather, the idea of "what hypnosis is" dictates how people react to it. Indeed, the results hypnosis produced, from twirling and shaking, to paralysis, to post hypnotic amnesia, and many other weird things changed depending on the times — the simple expectation of "what hypnosis was" influenced what hypnosis was.

In The *Origin of Consciousness in the Breakdown of the Bicameral Mind* Julian Jaynes argues that the reason hypnotherapists are able to use this "back door" into our minds is that there indeed is such a back door, and it was used all the time — either by religious leaders, shamans and the like, and, more controversially by our own "God voices" that told us what to do, which were really part of ourselves and our decision-making process, in the same way schizophrenics hear voices telling them what to do. To what degree this is factual I have no way of knowing, but I wager that there is a kernel of truth in it — this sort of "command override," which, when toggled, allows for a more direct control of our actions, which modern ideas of consciousness and free will simply get in the way of.

Indeed, the way we react to hypnosis, be it clinical or religious, and our susceptibility to trance-like states varies among cultures, and the methods of induction and the results differ depending on what the cultural norms are. As such, it is not too hard to imagine that if it was the norm to hear commands from gods and the voices of demons and angels, as many early peoples claim to have heard, such as those mentioned in the *Iliad* and the Epic of Gilgamesh, that such auditory and perhaps visual hallucinations would be common and considered ordinary at the time. Thinking things through and introspection might also be recent inventions: I do not mean to imply that previously people were non-thinking buffoons, but rather that the decisions arose without conscious effort, which is more or less how we lead our lives today in any case — we don't go into deep deliberations over which bag of potato chips to buy or what to do if a crazed solipsist starts running towards us. Only in the later parts of the *Iliad* did the first mentions of "human decision deliberation" begin to appear, in texts which are reputed to have been written later. Indeed, in those texts, the characters are surprised to have thought those thoughts, implying it was not common at the time. God-commands were taken at face value: in the Iliad, if someone told someone else that some particular god commanded them to do something, it was not met with recommendations of a mental institution, but with complete trust. Indeed, the notion that there was something wrong with you if you were hearing voices arose surprisingly late, and roughly coincides with the popularization of monotheism — suddenly, it was no longer in vogue to be your own prophet, and you could be executed for diverging from the "real" religion. Of course, this is a gross oversimplification, and further research is required.

Being under the influence of hypnosis or of an equivalent control mechanism such as a personal god delusion does not mean that you are hallucinating: in one interesting set of experiments, described in *The Origin of Consciousness in the Breakdown of the Bicameral Mind*, subjects were hypnotized to believe that there was no chair in the middle of the room, and were asked to cross the room. The results were fascinating: they, contrary to our intuitions, avoided the chairs even though they claimed that there was no chair, and they merely "chose to walk that way" or confabulated other rationalizations. On the other hand, when volunteers were asked to simulate what would happen if a hypnotized subject was to walk through a room after being told that there was no chair, the "simulator" volunteers crashed into the chairs. This reveals a fascinating difference between what we think hypnosis can do — make us hallucinate, with what it actually makes us do — interpret the world differently, to set aside reason in favor of "trance logic" or "paralogic" depending on what you want to call it.

Another great example of confabulation is in V. S. Ramachandran's *Phantoms in the Brain* where there was a certain category of stroke victims that couldn't move one of their arms, but were never actually aware of it — instead, when asked to lift up their hands, they would concoct stories such as "I'm feeling kind of tired," "I just moved it," "I don't want to," "Here, see!" (while lifting up their paralyzed arm with their healthy arm).

Now, the reason why I gave this crash course of examples of hypnosis and stroke victims rationalizing away their issues is that there seems to be one central thing in common with them — there seems to be a desperate need in the mind to preserve this sense of self, of this stable worldview, and of coherence. If this coherence is challenged, either through brain damage, where we are unable to know that we can't move an appendage, or through the direct verbal input of a hypnotherapist, we desperately patch up our reality with the band aids of rationalization, desperately hoping that any contradictions won't be noticed, either by us or by our compatriots.[1] It is only when the balance of contradicting information is unbearable that we finally have a worldview change. Indeed, all of this is heavily reminiscent of religious people, who will jump through verbal hoops and do logical acrobatics to explain away the inconsistencies in their religious worldviews, and this urge to preserve our sense of self seems to be the only possible reason we have religious apologetics that, even though they don't stand up to scrutiny, never seem to die away and are presented over and over again — if it were a matter of mere factual correction, such as finding out that tomorrow's temperature is different to what was promised, the hypothesis of gods that religions present would have died away ages ago. As such, it is up to you to determine, when talking to a believer, how deeply entrenched his beliefs are, and know that confronting said beliefs is not a mere exercise in correcting some logical errors, but in most cases is a deeply personal and emotional undertaking for the believer which can shake up his entire ego — that is, his entire sense of self-worth, of his worldview. Indeed, I once heard a proverb that "If your salary depends on not understanding a particular fact, you can rest assured you will have difficulty grasping it" — this isn't the direct quote, but I find it quite illustrative: if your getting into heaven rests upon you not understanding what that pesky atheist is saying, chances are it will take a lot of effort from that atheist to convince you.

---

[1] Here I do not mean that we plot to delude ourselves, this is but a metaphor to describe how our minds present us a clear, but sometimes false reality.

UNDERSTANDING OCCAM'S RAZOR

Before we move on to the Counter-Apologetics chapter, I must familiarize you with "Occam's Razor," since this term will be used often in future chapters. We can use it to show that "God did it!" types of claims are useless and that in fact they raise more questions than answers.

Among competing hypotheses, the hypothesis with the fewest assumptions should be selected. As such, the "simplest" explanation is preferable. "God" is not a simple explanation — a "God" would be infinitely complex and intricate.

Example: A cup in your house was knocked over. You have a cat. Which, in order, is the most likely?

A. A burglar knocked it over.
B. Your cat knocked it over.
C. God knocked it over.

Answer: B, A, C

Here, even if we haven't yet found out about evolution, a "god" would still be the least likely explanation for why there is life, since God, according to believers, is "infinitely complex," definitely more complex than all of life combined. Using God to explain anything at all would mean the use of an even bigger mystery to explain a smaller mystery. I could make up any number wild hypotheses such as, "Life is formed spontaneously when stars explode," and even that would actually be more probable due to the fact that stars are not infinitely complex. Of course, even my new pseudo-theory of AstroGenesis would still require some sort of evidence to be taken seriously.

COUNTER-APOLOGETICS

First, what are apologetics exactly? Let's consult our trusty dictionary![1]

Apologetics

1. The branch of theology that is concerned with defending or proving the truth of Christian doctrines.
2. Formal argumentation in defense of something, such as a position or system.

Disclaimer: In this and the proceeding chapters many apologetics arguments will have "example dialogues." Some of these dialogues are based on real dialogues but shortened for the purposes of this book; some are merely the counter-apologetic, in its simplest form, written for illustrative purposes. No two religious discussions are alike, and each dialogue is designed to best showcase that particular argument and how to counter it. Treat them as you

---

[1] www.thefreedictionary.com/apologetics

would dialogues in language-learning textbooks: they are meant to teach the specific point, sometimes at the price of brevity and oversimplification.

Pascal's wager

You may have heard of the mathematician and philosopher Blaise Pascal. While he had many extraordinary accomplishments in mathematics and physics, his "wager" unfortunately has much less merit.

Pascal posits that it is best to believe in God, since if he does exist you'll be rewarded with Heaven (infinite gain), while if he doesn't, you haven't lost much (finite loss). On the other hand, if you don't believe and God does exist, you will experience an infinite loss (hell).

	God exists	**God does not exist**
Belief	infinite gain	finite loss
Disbelief	infinite loss	finite gain

This argument is a step up from "the blatant threat of hell," which we'll discuss next, in that it's not as blatant, however just as with that argument, the fact that there are thousands of contradicting denominations/religions renders this argument useless. Also the notion that God would be as foolish as to accept someone's professed belief on account of it being "statistically beneficial" is insulting not only to our intelligence, but to the intelligence of the supposedly omniscient deity.

Threats of hell

This is the simplest apologetic, where you are told that you will go to hell if you don't believe in the particular deity that the believer professes. It goes something like this:

> You: But... I don't believe.
> Believer: Then you'll go to Hell!!!

One thing that the believers always seem to forget when presenting this argument, is that their religion is not the only one, and that even in the US there are thousands of different denominations of Christianity alone, many of which claim that they are the only true path. Even if one of them was correct, you'd still end up in hell due to the statistical improbability of picking the correct doctrine.

Overly sheltered theists that have never talked to an atheist, or don't really understand that atheists don't believe in gods, hells or heavens might raise this question. After overcoming your initial disbelief regarding the utter ignorance of this question, one must remind oneself that not everyone has had access to the same information that you have, and here it's best to keep things simple without being openly patronizing. This argument can be rephrased in various ways, such as "But what if you're wrong and you'll go to hell?" — phrasing it in that way at least makes it have a semblance of a logical argument, where the previous one is basically a "hell threat," however don't be fooled, since both are equally vapid. The fear of hell may persist in atheists even after deconversion for quite a while — some people suffer for years or decades (I was lucky to suffer only for a month, maybe several), after the emotional part of you catches up with the logical part, you will be as afraid of hell as you are of Darth Vader or the Boogie monster.

Rick: But aren't you afraid you'll go to hell?

Jett: Which one in particular? Is it one of the numerous of Christian hells that arose from having all of the different Christian denominations? Is it the Islamic hell? Is it the Hellenic underworld? How much thought, honestly, have you given to the thought of going to Muslim hell? It is the same apathy that you feel right now regarding being tortured in Muslim hell that I feel towards all hells in general.[1]

Rick: But what if one turns out to be real?

Jett: Well, due to the sheer number of hells, if one would indeed turn out to be real, it would likely not be the one that you are afraid of, and you would go to the "real" hell simply due to the statistical improbability of picking the "right" religion.

And if all else fails:

Jett: This reminds me of a parable: there once was a bunny rabbit — he would hop around merrily all day.

However, on one particular day, a group of scared-looking bunny rabbits approached him. "Don't you know that hopping around so merrily during daytime is bad," they said? The rabbit, looking perplexed, asked: "no, why? I've been hopping around in this manner all my life." The scared rabbits retorted "By hopping around so merrily, you will anger the carrots, and they will never grow again!" And so, with this new found knowledge, the rabbit never hopped in this merry fashion again.

---

[1] The above response was inspired by Sam Harris's reply in one of his question and answer sessions.

The argument from design

> *"Will you just look at the trees and the clouds, the beautiful butterflies — there is just no way all of this could have happened by chance"*
>
> *"I was walking down the beach, and saw a beautifully designed watch lying in the sand — it is then that I realized that everything else around me, like the trees and sand, was too, designed, like that watch"*
>
> *"Just like planes and cars have designers, everything else in nature was designed as well"*

The argument from design is formulated like so:

Look at (a building/mobile phone/ watch/plane/etc.) *— just as it is obvious that it has a designer and the notion that it all came about randomly is absurd, so it is just as absurd to claim that beautiful natural forms also came about randomly — so there must be a designer for them as well.*

This type of argument can be attacked from several directions. Indeed, one doesn't even need knowledge of evolution or cosmology to disprove it: one way is to tell the believer, "Okay, let's say we don't know anything about evolution or that such a concept even exists." The burden of proof for the existence of the "designer" still falls on the person making the claim, especially considering that claiming an "infinitely complex designer" for a "finitely complex creation" is in clear violation of Occam's Razor.

Language is our enemy here, I'm afraid, since words such as "Design" and "Creation" are very easy to abuse — even scientists often speak of how "evolution designed something," although evolution is not a conscious process. Don't allow yourself to be tricked by word games — we know that buildings and watches are designed, since we have pretty solid evidence of the existence of engineers, watchmakers and construction sites; however, saying that "everything" is designed makes the word lose its meaning. We do not "know" that someone designed the sand and the trees, and indeed we have pretty solid evidence to the contrary. Just Google how sand occurs[1] (hint: it happens naturally).

Revisiting the argument from design

The other route to refuting this claim is by explaining the theory of evolution to your debater. Of course, you are not a biologist.

[1] http://asdfscience.com/why-is-there-sand-on-beaches/

The first thing that someone might throw at you is the whole "evolution is just a theory" routine — this plays on the difference between the scientific and day-to-day usage of the word "theory":

> Common usage: "I have a theory that he is angry with me because I spilled coffee on him yesterday."

> Scientific usage: "I did a lot of testing of the merits of my hypothesis, and since my observations did not contradict the predictions of my hypothesis, I think it can soon be made into a theory."

As such, the scientific usages of the word "theory," found, for instance, in "the theory of gravity" and "the theory of evolution" are different from the layman's usage of which means "guess" or "interesting idea."

Of course, I will not offer a Biology 101 course to you here — Amazon has plenty of biology textbooks. Rather, I'll just give you some juicy comebacks for what those mean theists might tell you — since that's what you're here for and I'm all for not wasting your time.

The theory of evolution would never predict the spontaneous random creation of complex life forms, which is what creationists imply; rather it's a very slow change of minor details in a population over time. Among a population, of, say, pigeons, there is always some difference among the members of that species — some have slightly longer feathers, some have slightly stronger beaks, some may be fatter or thinner, and so forth — those minute differences do, however, gradually accumulate if they are beneficial — so if the pigeons without those features are less successful (can't mate or die early), their genes are simply not passed on. This is why there are no pigeons prone to fainting, and why people generally experience good health up to their 30s or 40s, and after that begin to decline — they have already passed on their genes so their genetic "warranty," if you will, has expired.

The argument from faith

"My ultimate proof for the existence of God is my faith."

When all else fails, this is the theist's last resort, their unassailable bastion with which they hope to end the discussion and hope that you will just nod and switch to another topic. However, the notion that "faith is a virtue" is false.

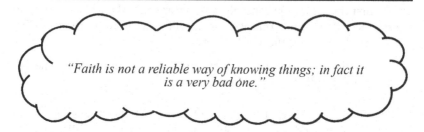

"Faith is not a reliable way of knowing things; in fact it is a very bad one."

In English, we have two words with similar meanings — "faith" and "belief." In Slavic languages such as Russian and Ukrainian there is no such distinction, and we just have one word, "belief." In English, "faith" seems to be reserved for the more "ethereal" beliefs and religion, while "belief" is more commonly used for down-to-earth things, such as "I believe it is going to rain tomorrow."

If he were told that faith is not a reliable way of knowing things, the theist might retort that everyone has faith — for instance the faith that the sun will come up tomorrow. This is a false comparison, as we have good understanding of the natural laws that make the earth rotate around the sun, as well as our experience of the sun rising up every morning. So, we do not need faith for that. Faith is a very slippery word, and I'd avoid it at all costs in debates. Instead, when people mention faith, try to dissect what they mean by it and replace it with this phrase:

I think that _____ corresponds to reality with a certainty of _____% because of the following evidence_____.

Of course, this is nowhere near as poetic as "faith," but at least here the discussion can actually commence.

The biggest issue with faith as "The proof for God" is this: which god does it prove? There are roughly 4,200 religions in the world, according to Wikipedia,[1] and that doesn't include all of the different denominations — of which there are several thousand Christian ones in the US alone. I'm sure every follower of those religions can use the same exact faith argument, even though they contradict each other on basic things such as the amount of gods, and often promise the bad kind of afterlife to the adherents of the other "improper" faiths. As such, the argument from faith is completely useless.

Peter Boghossian, in his book *A Manual for Creating Atheists*, argues that the best way to challenge other people's beliefs, instead of getting bogged down in discussions of scripture or other matters (trust me, I've indeed been bogged down in such discussions that took up hours and hours, only to end at an impasse), is to instead attack the "root" of the problem, that is faith, and to shift the discussion back towards the fallibility of faith, if the subject attempts to shift the conversation towards something to the effect of "faith gives me hope."

---

[1]   http://en.wikipedia.org/wiki/List_of_religions_and_spiritual_traditions

"We fear clear, honest, blunt dialogue, but what we ought to fear are stupid and dangerous ideas, because while blunt and honest dialogue might be offensive to some, stupid and dangerous ideas can be fatal to all of us."
—Matt Thornton, community activist

Fundamentally, when debating a theist, one has to deal with not just a simple set of facts, which, if corrected, would change the person's views, but the entire way that the person thinks. This "Way of knowing" is called epistemology. While there are many different types of epistemology, the two we will need to distinguish between will be:

• Religious Faith — "belief without evidence," or even "belief despite of evidence," and as Peter Boghossian put it "pretending to know things that you don't know."

• The Scientific Method — a method of research in which a problem is identified, relevant data are gathered, a hypothesis is formulated, and the hypothesis is empirically tested.[1]

As I mentioned previously, English is actually lucky in that there is a distinction between "faith" and "belief," wherein "faith" is used more when talking about spiritual matters and "belief" is more generalized. On the other hand, languages like Russian and Ukrainian have just a single word "vera/vira." As such, the sentence that looked so impressive in English become nonsensical when translated to such a language where there is just a single word for "belief":

Faith — "Belief without evidence."
Belief — "Belief without evidence."

To combat this, and to demystify these terms even in English, I prefer to either replace the term "faith/belief" with something more precise, or use qualifiers, for instance "religious faith" or "spiritual faith." Again, it can be useful throw out the words faith and belief entirely and replace them with this incredible sentence:

I regard ____ as corresponding to reality/the real world with ____% confidence, based on the evidence of _____.

This formulation intentionally cripples all of the poetic obfuscations that allow apologists to conflate faith and actual reasoned knowing.

Examples:

I regard Jesus as described in the Bible as corresponding to reality/the real world with 100% confidence, based on the evidence of the Bible.

---

[1] From http://www.thefreedictionary.com/

> I regard *The divinity of the Bible* as corresponding to reality/the real world with 100% confidence, based on the evidence of the Bible.
>
> I regard *The divinity of the Quran* as corresponding to reality/the real world with 100% confidence, based on the evidence of the Quran.
>
> I regard *Aliens somewhere in the universe* as corresponding to reality/the real world with 100% confidence, based on the evidence of the Drake equation.
>
> I regard *Getting to work on time tomorrow* as corresponding to reality/the real world with 25% confidence, based on the evidence of my previous week.

A "trump card" that theists might attempt to use in their feeble attempt to justify their position is that apparently "religious faith" and "the scientific method" essentially have the same merit, since just as they have faith in their religion, you have "faith in science." This is false. The scientific method is the polar opposite of faith: whereas adherents of religious faiths have no self-correcting method for deciding which doctrine or belief is the correct one, and indeed questioning tenets of "the faith" can get you excommunicated, shunned, labeled as immoral or even executed, adherents of science have no such qualms: indeed, if you were to show how a widely accepted scientific concept is false, you would be lauded as a genius, and possibly be given the Nobel Prize. Indeed, for something to be considered "scientific," a mere "revelation" is not enough, and neither is discovering something in a laboratory: the results have to be reproducible — if you discover some marvelous new thing, say "the cure for aging in mice," and claim that your mice can live for several decades or more, you would have to publish how exactly you accomplished such a feat, and these results would then have to be reproduced in various laboratories around the world, and only then would you have any real credibility. Contrast that with "mystical" ways of gaining longevity.

If you wish to publish an article in a scientific journal, it has to be peer-reviewed, which means that people from your field will be randomly selected by the journal, and will anonymously attempt to bash your idea and poke as many holes in it as they can. Only if it holds up will it be published. Creationists (people that believe that the earth is 4,000 — 6,000 years old) have gone around this by creating their own special journals where they publish their articles and papers without interference from those pesky "real scientists."

One does not need to "have faith in science": in many debates, a theist might bring up an obscure scientific issue such as "quantum mechanics" or "the beginning of the universe," and imply that since you do not understand a specific scientific field, you could not possibly argue with him, since he has all the answers. This is false. You do not need to know "all of the sciences" to be able to argue theology. All you need is a basic understanding of the scientific method and its advantages over how religious faith works.

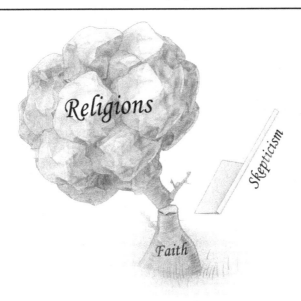

Religions

Skepticism

Faith

Cut down the tree of Faith with Skepticism, and the Religions will fall

Unlike conversions to a religion, a "deconversion" does not usually occur after a single conversation (unless the person was on the "brink" already and needed someone to "give him permission" to deconvert or "the final push"). The most you can usually hope for is to give your interlocutor a new direction of thought, which he, in his own time, may follow. This may take months or years, or it may never occur.

In *A Manual for Creating Atheists*, Peter Boghossian notes that contrary to popular belief, if the conversation ends with the theist becoming emotional or angry, this is actually a good thing, and often times after having ended the conversation on very bad terms, the same person would months later call him back to thank him. It is your job, however, to remain steady and supportive throughout the discussion. It is fine if you seem "disrespectful" towards their system of belief, as long as it is grounded on rationality. It is important too that the subject does not sense any frustration or anger from you, since that would place you in the role of "rival debater" — rather, the behavioral and emotional model that you should try to mimic would be that of getting someone to quit drinking or using drugs: you should be supportive towards the person, but merciless towards the beliefs.

It is worth watching "The Atheist Experience" [1] to get a sense of how to talk to theists. The strategies on the show vary, however, and many would not be applicable when talking to a person whom you can't simply stop talking to on the phone and with whom one might wish further discourse. The show, which is available for free at their website, is an invaluable resource for all up-and-coming atheists, and I have to admit to having watched practically

---

[1] www.atheist-experience.com

all of their available episodes — it was just so refreshing, at that stage in my deconversion, to have seen something so different to what I was used to.

You will find many religious debates up on YouTube — those are an invaluable resource if you are new to atheism. I had a great time watching them, however such debates (for instance, Richard Dawkins, author of "*The God Delusion*," standing on a stage debating some apologist or another), are not representative of the discussions that regular people have. For one thing, the style of discourse (each side being given a certain amount of time, then an equal amount of time for a response), is simply not how regular discussions work. I have also found that after a while, the content of such formalized debates (an atheist and theist debating in front of an audience) is very repetitive, and neither the atheist nor theist expects to convince each other — rather, they aim to sway the audience as well as sell their books afterwards.

Seek out less formal debate videos, such as those offered by the Magic Sandwich Show and the Jinn and Tonic Show channels.

To avoid getting bogged down in a discussion about specific aspects of one religion or another, I recommend this simple two-step heuristic:
1. Whatever the religious person is proclaiming, lead them towards acknowledging that their opinion is based on faith.
2. Explain why faith is not a reliable form of epistemology, and ask them to "do more research about their beliefs" (the "Graceful Exit").

Two steps? It seems as if it should be more complicated, but it really isn't.

The ontological argument

The ontological argument can be phrased in various ways, but the bare essence is as follows:
1. God can be summarized as the ultimate, perfect being; anything greater cannot be conceived.
2. Beings that are ultimate and perfect also include the property of existing — otherwise they wouldn't be perfect.
3. Therefore, God exists.

The objection to this argument is that, by its logic, "anything that we define as awesome must include the property of existing, and therefore it exists," that is, we are just defining things into existence. The best way to counter this argument is with counter examples:
4. Santa Claus can be summed up as the most awesome, kindest, hardest working, gift giving individual.
5. Beings that are "the most awesome" also include the property of existing — otherwise they wouldn't be the most awesome.
6. Therefore, Santa Claus exists.

You can create as many examples as you want, using fictional characters, places, and events to demonstrate the uselessness of this argument. Furthermore, even if this argument were to magically become valid, it would at best prove "some undefined god."

If presented with this argument, after answering it, please inquire if this argument in particular was the thing that convinced the theist to believe — chances are that it's not, and the theist simply found it on some apologetics website or on a course on converting people. Inquire the true and "most salient" reason for their faith and go after that instead.

The "argument from degree," which we will discuss soon, is a variation of this argument.

The natural-law argument

"The physical universe has consistent and predictable laws — as such, there should be a law giver."

First of — which God? Allah? The flying spaghetti monster? By saying, "Look — we have all of these natural laws which make life and the universe possible — therefore God," one asserts that a god, which by most definitions is even more complex than the universe which it supposedly created, is the reason, and this goes against all scientific knowledge of how things come into existence, where in things are at first simple, and gradually become more complex, and falls foul of Occam's Razor, where in the explanation with the fewest possible assumptions is the preferred explanation, assuming equal evidence for both versions of events — and we have plenty more evidence for the scientific version.

This argument also relies on the ambiguous usage of the word "law." By law we can mean either prescriptive laws, such as "thou shalt not kill," or descriptive laws, such as those used by scientists to describe the world around us. These "natural laws" are tools that humans use to describe the universe, and as we find out more about how things work, we write down more such laws. We happen to call both types "laws," however we just as easily could have had a different word such as "gtuil" to describe human laws and "liom" to describe natural laws, and if we were used to differentiating them verbally, no such equivocation would have occurred.

To blast this argument away once and forever, and impress everyone, get to know the Euthyphro Dilemma:

> *"Why did God issue just those natural laws and no others? If you say that he did it simply from his own good pleasure, and without any reason, you then find that there is something which is not subject to law, and so your train of natural law is interrupted. If you say, as more orthodox theologians do, that in all the laws which God issues he had a reason for giving those laws rather than others — the reason, of course, being to create the best universe, although you would never think it to look at it — if there was a reason for the laws which God gave, then God himself was subject to law, and therefore you do not get any advantage by introducing God as an intermediary."*
>
> — *Bertrand Russell*

The Euthyphro Dilemma is discussed in more detail in the chapter "Atheism and Morality," but the short version is that if a god "thought up" the morality, then it is his subjective view and not absolute/objective, and if morality is somehow ingrained in the universe and a god informs us of it, then that god does not seem as important all of a sudden. If a god "always existed" with that morality, then he didn't choose it and it might just as well be random.

The "just look at the trees!" argument

This is a variant of the argument from design, wherein, impressed by the wonders of nature, you are supposed to conclude that they must have been created by God. Furthermore, it is surely the one god that the person making the argument believes in, not any other ("weird") god. Of course, there is no actual evidence that all of the wonders of nature came into existence due to their god, and the concept of evolution is still the best available explanation to account for the similarities we can see in the broad array of organisms that have existed over time.

I initially was content with implying that all that was needed was "further education regarding evolution," and that creationists are merely "misinformed." However, my editor was quick to point out that it's not that simple: sure, some folks merely lack even the basic knowledge of evolution and some educating would do good to their benighted minds. However, some compartmentalize, accepting evolution in some cases, such as the evolution of animals or bacteria, while cordoning off the world of evolution from humans, since humans are "special" and "distinct," and in no way are we merely animals. Funny how the religious can then claim to be humble with a straight face.

Another implication of this argument, if it were actually true, is that the god in question must also have created all the bad things as well, for instance mosquitoes, Ebola and taxes.

Believers may attempt to counter this "creation of bad things" argument by claiming that without "evil" there would be no "free will." It is highly likely that those same believers would have a hard time describing what free will actually is — for more on that read the chapter named "Free Will." While our free will may suffer if we were magically prevented from doing bad things (or any things for that matter), it is already bound in a myriad of other ways: we can't fly without the aid of machinery, sustain ourselves by eating furniture or live in outer space without life support systems, or use telekinesis. All of those things hinder our ability to impact on the world, yet we still have free will.

The "you must pray and answers/faith will come!" argument

During debates with theists, if their logical arguments fail due to your extreme experience in counter-apologetics, this is one of the arguments they'll use to finish the conversation. Certainly, if you say "No, I won't pray, it's silly," they'll accuse you of being closed-minded; on the other hand, if you DO pray, and nothing comes of it, it is merely your "lack of faith" and you should continue praying.

The problem here is with the premise — how would they feel (assuming they are Christians) if you DID pray, and a few days later announced, "Indeed, my prayers were successful — I prayed towards Mecca and Allah came before me, and now I believe." In pushing the notion that you should pray, they automatically pre-suppose that their particular religion is the correct one and that if a positive result does occur, it will be for their exact type of religion. There is also no way to "prove them wrong": if you succeed and become spiritual, they are correct, and if you don't, then they still are not wrong since according to their worldview you just need to have more faith. Perhaps, one way out of this would be to have them read any of the numerous books which were written to deconvert believers, in return for which you would pray earnestly for five minutes for a few days — surely a chance to save a soul is worth reading a silly atheist book?

If that didn't work, another way would be to ask them to pray for you, since you obviously do not have enough faith, so surely it is up to them to have God enlighten your soul — after all, their arguments couldn't convince you, and your praying didn't help either; so every time they try to bother you, just ask them to pray for you instead.

"So many people believe X, can they all be wrong?"

Yes, indeed they can. For the longest time, folks believed that the sun revolved around the earth, and that the earth was flat. The same argument can be thrown back at them since most people on the planet do not hold the same belief as they do. Even Christianity (which, if you include all the ever-increasing subdivisions and offshoots, is the largest religion on the planet) counts fewer "believers" than "everyone else."

Scientists, doctors and the like are not applicable to this fallacy — if 99 of 100 astronomers believe that the earth revolves around the sun, then, since they are the folks who have devoted their lives to the study of said matter, it would be safe to trust them, on account of their using the scientific method and all that other sciency goodness. The problem only arises when the population at large is questioned about something that it can't really claim to know — think of polling an entire city on a question regarding the migration of pigeons. Their answers simply won't hold much merit in comparison to a poll conducted among pigeon experts.

"But!!..." the theist might argue, "the scientist is not qualified to answer questions about God as well! His domain is that of the material and not of the spiritual."

If that is the case however, this would mean that their version of God would be of the non-intervening kind, meaning that things like answered prayers and miracles would not exist since those things are all part of the material world and can be tested for, and as such, their god would be indistinguishable from a god that does not exist.

Exercise Time! (Counter-Apologetics Part 1)

Think up a brief response:
1. I know God exists because I have faith.

2. But aren't you afraid that you'll go to hell if you are wrong?

3. God can be summarized as the ultimate, perfect being, anything greater cannot be conceived. Beings that are ultimate and perfect also include the property of existing — otherwise they wouldn't be perfect. Therefore, God exists.

"There are scientists who believe in God."

There indeed are scientists who believe in God. However, they all mostly believe in the gods of their specific cultures: it would have been mighty impressive if, once you became a scientist in India, for example, you shrugged off your Hindu beliefs and became a Christian. Indeed, even in the religious United States, more than 70% of scientists do not believe, while only around 10–20% of the general population are non-religious.

Scientists are expected to put away their religious views when doing actual sciency stuff, since their religious views can only at best be classified as wobbly hypothesis with no real evidence. It matters highly what type of scientist you are: for instance, if you are an evolutionary biologist it would be very weird indeed if you were also a creationist, and at best I could see evolutionary biologists as believing in some sort of ethereal deistic, non-interfering god, not the type that causes worldwide floods and creates the earth in 6 days (for on the 7th, he rested). On the other hand, if you are, say, a rocket scientist, then your field of study doesn't directly intersect with things written in the Bible. Wait — I'm wrong — since according to the Bible the Sky/Heavens are a half sphere on which the stars are glued on to — or are they holes? I'm not sure, and the earth is flat and stands on columns. Hmm yeah, so unless you believe in a highly modernized version of the Bible that has been interpreted to fit today's knowledge, it would be weird for any educated person to believe in such a thing.

There is a related argument you might hear about how Albert Einstein believed in God, and some nice quotes as well to seemingly substantiate it such as:

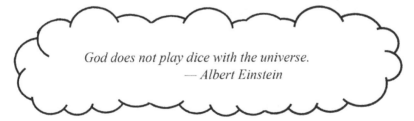

God does not play dice with the universe.
— Albert Einstein

This quote is indeed by him, however here again we stumble on the vagueness of the term "God." If the believer in question that is presenting this argument would bother to do a few minutes' worth of googling, he would soon realize that Albert Einstein is considered by most to have been a pantheist, which means that he did not believe in an anthropomorphic or personal god and considered such notions childish, rather he held a poetic "God is the Universe" type of belief. He also labeled himself as "agnostic" and "religious nonbeliever." [1] He was also skeptical about any notions of an afterlife. In essence, he was a nonbeliever but felt that only religiosity could provide that awe, that wonder of the universe — too bad he lived before Carl Sagan. Finally, to slam the door shut on this subject, let's hear from Albert Einstein himself after he was asked about this matter, since Albert Einstein is a great authority on Albert Einstein:

> *"It was, of course, a lie what you read about my religious convictions, a lie which is being systematically repeated. I do not believe in a personal God and I have never denied this but have expressed it clearly. If something is in me which can be called religious then it is the unbounded admiration for the structure of the world so far as our science can reveal it."*
>
> *- Albert Einstein*

> *"The word God is for me nothing more than the expression and product of human weaknesses, the Bible a collection of honorable, but still primitive legends. No interpretation no matter how subtle can (for me) change this. These subtilised interpretations are highly manifold according to their nature and have almost nothing to do with the original text."*
>
> *- Albert Einstein*

In the end though, even if Albert Einstein or some other great inventor or scientist were to believe in one god or another, it wouldn't really matter if those beliefs were not substantiated by scientific facts — they might as well perform great scientific discoveries while believing in fairies or dragons. What matters is that the discovery itself is useful, not the other, sometimes misguided beliefs of the discoverer which do not have any impact on that discovery.

The extreme amounts argument, also known as the "argument from degree"

Thomas Aquinas, who was a Roman Catholic theologian, wrote a work called "Summa Theologica." In it rests, among others, this argument:

---

[1] Religious views of Albert Einstein:
http://en.wikipedia.org/wiki/Religious_views_of_Albert_Einstein

*We notice that things in the world differ. There are degrees of, say, goodness or per-
fection. But we judge these degrees only by comparison with a maximum. Humans
can be both good and bad, so the maximum goodness cannot rest in us. Therefore
there must be some other maximum to set the standard for perfection, and we call
that maximum God.*

A syllogistic form collected by Robert J. Schihl follows:

1. Objects have properties to greater or lesser extents.
2. If an object has a property to a lesser extent, then there exists some
   other object that has the property to the maximum possible degree.
3. So there is an entity that has all properties to the maximum possible
   degree.
4. Hence God exists.

There is an immediate problem with the second part of the argument: as
Richard Dawkins in his book *The God Delusion* bluntly stated, if that were so,
then there should therefore exist an object with the maximum amount of
smelliness.

The third part of the argument is a complete non sequitur (it does not
logically follow) — how did we suddenly get to a deity?

By the way, the god we learn about in the Old Testament is hardly "the
maximum of all goodness"; he has a penchant for wholesale slaughters,
flooding the entire earth and torturing people for an eternity for committing
finite crimes.

Even if we somehow got past that to #4, "Hence God exists" — which
god? Allah? Vishnu?

The extreme amounts argument is more or less the ontological argument
but dressed up somewhat differently.

The argument from morality

This one, in its simplest syllogistic form, says:

1. Morality requires God to exist.
2. Morality exists.
3. Therefore God Exists.

We will instantly take issue with the first premise: who can prove a
God is required for morality to exist? And if so — which God in particular?
Zeus? Morality is an ability that humans and other social mammals acquired
through evolution — indeed many other animals including chimpanzees

and elephants exhibit some simpler forms of morality, since it is highly beneficial for the survival of social mammals which live in groups. Clearly, those people who claim that only humans have morality need to watch more nature documentaries.

I can also take some issue with Number 2 — here, an "absolute" type of morality is meant, as if the universe were a computer game with hard-coded conditions for winning. On the other hand, it has yet to be proven that a morality that is wired into the fabric of the cosmos exists. We humans and some other social animals have what's known as an inter-subjective morality, meaning that large populations can have a coherent and similar understanding of what's good and bad — of course there are outliers and everyone has his own take on morality, but nearly all of us have a general "common core" of morality, and know not to stray too far from it or face the legal ramifications.

The third part of the argument "Therefore God Exists" does not tell us which god in particular it is talking about — is it the Flying Spaghetti Monster?

A holy book is not evidence of god(s)

Oftentimes, when talking to believers, they will either attempt to bring up their holy book or bring up a particular verse, passage, or chapter of said text. Just because something is written in an ancient text doesn't make it true — think of the *Iliad*, *The Epic of Gilgamesh*, the numerous ancient Greek/Roman legends, and all of the competing religions that the believer conveniently ignores. Whenever you are confronted with "scriptural evidence," dig into why the believer ignores all of the other ancient texts. If you get brushed off with the theist claiming that "it is all supported by historical evidence," continue inquiring about that evidence — there has of yet been no scientifically-verified evidence of anything supernatural ever occurring in history... ever!

The historicity of the Bible is spotty to say the least. The first texts mentioning Jesus were written from a few decades to several hundred years after the date he was supposedly crucified.[1] Whether a prophet called Jesus existed at that time and place we will probably never know, since so many elements of his story, such as the virgin birth, performing miracles, the shooting star signifying his birth, the "wise men," and others, are also found in accounts of previous prophets like Zoroaster. The Bible that we have with us today was put together during the Nicean Council in CE 325, where early Christians decided which separate books (which the Bible is now comprised of) would become parts of the official doctrine and which were to be considered "Apocrypha" — and the amount of "Apocrypha" is larger than the content of the Bible, and a lot of it is quite amusing to read.

If you continue to receive claims that the "holy book" is historically

---

[1] http://en.wikipedia.org/wiki/Historical_reliability_of_the_Gospels

accurate:

• Remind them that people from other religions have the same exact claims, and ask how you can differentiate between these claims.

• Point to the "Historical Method." [1]

• And ask them to do their own research before continuing this conversation (the "Graceful Exit").

> Bob: You've given me some interesting points — however, all of the answers you need are in the Bible. If you read it, you will become wiser.

> Mogu: If I read it — what sort of answers would I get? How would they change my position?

> Bob: You will see that the Lord really loves you, and if you accept him into your heart you will be blessed.

> Mogu: Right, but as far as actual historicity goes, how is it more valid than the other several thousands of religions that humans know of?

> Bob: The Bible has deep historical roots.

> Mogu: Actually, no — the initial texts that the Bible is comprised of were written during a period from a few decades A.D. to a few hundred years A.D. Also many of the great events in the Bible, such as the great worldwide flood[2] and Jews building the pyramids never happened.[3] If anything, the Quran is more historical since there, the passage of information about that tradition was documented.

> Bob: What do you mean, the Jews didn't build the pyramids?

> Mogu: There are no Egyptian accounts of this — and Egyptians kept pretty good records. The gravesites found near the pyramids indicate that they were built by skilled Egyptian laborers that were well fed, drank wine, and were well-compensated overall. I know this may come as new and unexpected information, so we can take a break and you can research this on your own. ("Graceful Exit.")

---

[1] http://en.wikipedia.org/wiki/Historical_method
[2] A great flood, or indeed maybe several great floods, may indeed have occurred for that region, with accounts such as Ziusudra, Gilgamesh, and Atrahasis that predate the Torah. However there is no evidence for a "worldwide" flood. Still, for those involved in the flood, it may as well have seemed to encompass the known world.
[3] http://en.wikipedia.org/wiki/The_Exodus

The argument from ignorance

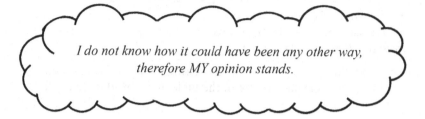

*I do not know how it could have been any other way,
therefore MY opinion stands.*

Common Usage:

1. I cannot conceive of the universe originating in any way other than through God.
2. I had a fatal disease that was impossible to cure, but I prayed and was cured, so it could only have been God that cured me.

The problem with this type of reasoning is that "not knowing any other way that something could have happened" does not automatically make your explanation correct. In order for your explanation to hold any weight it would be required that you could actually provide some evidence in its favor — otherwise anything goes: it could have been aliens that cured you, and this entire universe could be a computer simulation within someone's dream who is actually a tadpole.

When dealing with this logical fallacy, I recommend against naming it, as the believer might misunderstand it and feel offended as if he himself is being called ignorant — instead explain its essence.

Dialog 1

> John: The universe is so complex — there is simply no way that it could have come about randomly, so this is why I think it was created by God.

> Allen: Which one in particular?

> John: The God of the Bible.

> Allen: Why not Allah or Shiva?

Dialog 2

> John: The universe is so complex — there is simply no way that it could have come about randomly, so this is why I think it was created by God.

> Storyteller: You know, this reminds me of an old story — Two bunny rabbits were discussing how the sun came up every morning.

The first rabbit was adamant: "It is the giant sky carrot that pushes it upwards — surely there is no other way!" The second bunny rabbit was not so sure — he has never seen the giant sky carrot. "But it is made of light — it can't be seen" proclaimed the first rabbit. Both rabbits had no way to test either claim, so they went back to eating grass, and were later themselves eaten by a fox. That fox was later eaten by Sir Isaac Newton, who discovered gravity!

Dialog 3

John: The universe is so complex — there is simply no way that it could have come about randomly, so this is why I think it was created by God.

Storyteller: You know, this reminds me of something — I once had an aunt who had problems with diabetes — so bad was it, in fact, that the doctors said that if things didn't change soon, they'd have to amputate her leg. However, that very same day, she started meditating in front of special crystals that she claims have supernatural energy and emit special vibrations. In just under a month, her diabetes all but vanished and her leg is now totally fine. She claims that it could have been nothing else but the crystals — what do you think?

In the first of the above discussions we saw that the atheist never actually confronted the argument from ignorance itself, but rather went for clarifying which god in particular the theist believed in and why — not all logical fallacies need to be confronted, since believers often emit so many. Remember the goal — get to the discussion of faith and why it is a flawed method of epistemology (of knowing things). In the final two discussions, the atheist used analogies to explain the concept of the "argument from ignorance," since actually naming it might be counter-productive.

Liana: I had this fatal disease that was impossible to cure, but I prayed and therefore God cured me.

Drake: It is truly amazing that you're cured, and I'm really interested to know one thing...

Liana: Sure, what?

Drake: How do you know that it was indeed God, or not, say, luck, modern medicine, or indeed some other benevolent deity or intelligence?

Liana: I believe that it could only have been God.

Once it has been narrowed down to "belief," you can then go the usual route and explain why religious faith is a bad thing.

The watchmaker argument

"You are walking down the beach — all off a sudden you see a watch in the sand, and you know that it was designed. Just as a watch needs a watchmaker, a creation — that is, the universe, needs a Creator — God is that Creator."

We know that things such as buildings and airplanes have creators, since we have ample evidence to support that fact: turn on a good documentary and you are bound to see how a 747 is constructed. On the other hand, with human beings there is ample evidence to the contrary — that they reproduce and evolve naturally. We also have a pretty good idea how planets are formed as well. When it comes to the universe, we are still not totally sure — Lawrence Krauss's book *A Universe from Nothing* is a good layman's guide into the modern theories as to how that could have occurred.

If "everything is designed" — that is, both the grains of sand and the watch, then how was the person that made this argument able to distinguish between them? In that type of universe, what would something that is "not designed" look like? The word "designed" would become meaningless. This argument is but a version of "the argument from design" which was refuted earlier; however I find that re-refuting similar arguments in various ways is good practice. Either that or I wrote about the previous one first, forgot about it, and then wrote this — I prefer the first explanation.

The number of people who believe something doesn't matter.

Known as "argumentum ad populum," which is Latin for "appeal to the people," it means is that if even a huge amount of people believe something, it doesn't automatically make it so.

Dialog 1

Amanda: So you're saying all those billions of people who believe in God are wrong?

Bob: Not so long ago, the majority of Europeans believed in the ancient Greco-Roman gods, and that instead of blood, humans had the four humors: black bile, yellow bile, phlegm and blood, which corresponded to the four temperaments and a deficiency or excess in which would cause illness.

Amanda: But this is different!

Bob: So, the fact that many people believe something is not the issue then?

Dialog 2

James: Almost everyone believes in God — therefore he must exist!

Rick: Countless children believe in Santa Claus — are you saying they are all wrong?

The argument from authority

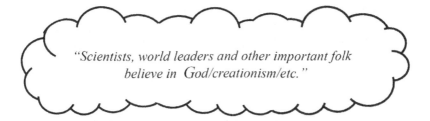

"*Scientists, world leaders and other important folk believe in God/creationism/etc.*"

The importance of the person in question who holds a particular belief doesn't lend credence to that belief. The only exception is if that person specializes in that field. For instance, if a geologist starts spouting off about how gods exist, we can safely ignore him. However if he and the geologist community overall have some new insight into how mountains are formed,[1] then we may trust their judgment.

Exercise Time! (Counter-Apologetics Part 2)

Think up a brief response:
1. Albert Einstein believed in God.
2. I do not know how the universe would have come into existence if not for God!
3. The Bible (Quran/Torah/Book of Mormon/Stuff I wrote yesterday) is the evidence for God!

"Don't you wish it was so?"

When all else fails, an emergency tactic disguised as an honest philosophical question is, "Don't you wish it was so?" Here, giving a yes or no answer is secondary to pointing out that wishing for something doesn't make it true.

---

[1] I think we already know pretty well how they are formed; this was just a random example.

Mark: Don't you wish there was an afterlife?

Jane: I wish for many things, but just wanting something hard enough doesn't automatically make it so: for instance, I wish to have a million dollars, and for there to be world peace — but just because "it would be great if that were the case" doesn't automatically validate the truthfulness of an idea.

Mark: Yes, but that is why you need faith.

Jane: This reminds me of a parable: there once was a cute fuzzy bunny rabbit, and all he wanted most in the entire world was to have a golden carrot. He searched and searched, and collected as many carrots as he could, and would attempt to transmute them into gold. Wish as he might though, the carrots would just rot and not turn into gold. Finally, the rabbit realized that the carrots won't turn into gold, and should be enjoyed for what they actually are.

Mark: I get your point, but why are you using such a childish analogy?

Jane: The simpler the analogy the better — this is what makes them memorable. The shock of it being so childish yet so deep at the same time will hopefully make it stick in your memory better.

The Kalam cosmological argument

1. Everything that begins to exist must have a cause.
2. The universe began to exist.
3. The universe must therefore have a cause.
4. That cause is God.

This is William Lane Craig's version of said argument — I posit this one in particular as it is able to get the essence across without excess verbiage. The "First Cause Argument" was actually created by Plato and Aristotle, and was later refined and morphed into the current, widely used variant, by Muslim philosophers and later by William Lane Craig.

Whenever you explore arguments that consist of "multiple points" (1. something something, 2. something something, 3. something else), it is helpful to go through them one by one. Let's do just that:

1. *Everything that begins to exist must have a cause.*

   — I'm not convinced. I have not seen "everything," and neither have you, so I don't know how you could make such an assumption.

2. *The universe began to exist.*

— Do we really know that? How do we define "universe"? Perhaps it existed in some other form prior to the Big Bang that we simply cannot comprehend?

3. *The universe must therefore have a cause.*

— Invalid due to the objections in point one and two.

4. *That cause is God.*

— How do we automatically jump to that conclusion? What if it is some weird natural explanation, perhaps something to do with quantum mechanics, or fairies for that matter, or magical universe-creating unicorns that are also mortal and therefore not gods?

As noted by Dan Barker, this argument sneakily divides everything into things that begin to exist and things that do not begin to exist. Somehow God gets a pass and is allowed into the "things that do not begin to exist" category — why is the universe not given that same privilege? What if the universe existed in some simpler or different form prior to the Big Bang, and therefore always existed and never "began to exist"?

The Judeo-Christian god is a being of infinite complexity, and as most theists will agree, more complex than the entire universe, and it's exactly God's über-complexity that comes back to haunt them in this argument: when we attempt to explain something complex by invoking something that is infinitely more complex, we are not actually explaining anything: it's like claiming fairies made the cup fall down instead of the cat. It is only if we knew the mechanisms by which a god would work and had a chance to observe and study how gods create universes, would we be able to say, with any degree of credibility that "yeah, maybe this 'gods that create universes' hypothesis is actually pretty neat" — otherwise, without any evidence, this explanation is no better than anything you can come up with using your imagination.

Finally, if we were to somehow dismiss all of these prior objections that demolish this argument; we would still left with the question of "which god?" The Muslims, which helped advance this argument, were clearly not doing this as a favor to Christians, but rather to advance their own beliefs in Allah. The fact that now both religions use this argument demonstrates its cardinal weakness: even if there were no objections to it, it would still only demonstrate the existence of "a god," but not any specific one.

Sensus Divinitatis a.k.a the "Sense of Divinity"

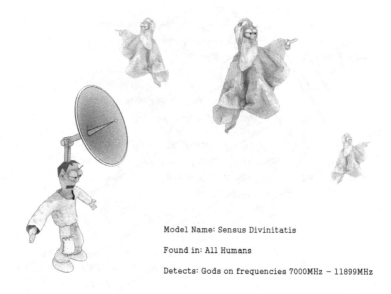

Model Name: Sensus Divinitatis

Found in: All Humans

Detects: Gods on frequencies 7000MHz – 11899MHz

"Everyone can sense that God exists deep down in their hearts."

A "sense of divinity" is a sense that every person supposedly has, that allows you to know of God. As such, people that argue for the existence of this sense imply that it is impossible for "true" atheists to exist, as everyone actually believes, deep down.

This may have worked fine on medieval peasants, who knew not of other religions, but for us folk here in the age of the Internet, it is quite obvious that there are numerous religions, each with their own ideas about God, including the number of gods, also may religions have other aspects, for instance demigods (half-gods), and all of these various theologies are totally inconsistent with each other. There are some rare exceptions though, such as the Bahai faith, according to which the other major religions are correct as well, but you won't find any religion that claims "Well you can come to this here temple, but that one across the street is actually more correct."

If this sense existed we would all be worshipping the same god and the rituals and rules would all be crystal-clear, no interpretations necessary. With the sheer number of various world religions, and the ever-growing amount of secular folk, this argument I feel is best left for the history books.

"There is a 'God part' of the brain, therefore God exists"

This argument is closely related to the previous "Sense of divinity." Researchers have previously been able to produce transcendent, highly spiritual feelings in individuals by stimulating certain regions of the brain. This region is also stimulated during some forms of epileptic seizures, so indeed it is not uncommon for epileptics whose seizures affect those same regions of the brain to have developed a distinct personality of spirituality, where everything seems ominous, godly and important. It seems therefore, that when the normal mechanism associated with assigning importance to things goes haywire, all of a sudden everything gets the "top importance" label.

Some newer articles, however, claim that there is no such single region, and that it is all much more complex, with different parts interacting and the person's religious predispositions mattering as well.

Regardless if there is a single region in the brain that causes godly feelings, or if it's the result of a complex interaction of different brain regions, or even something more complex, one should still inquire as to their meaning: the religious folks claim that it is proof of God, for why else would there be need for such a thing? This is the classic argument from ignorance however, and is like saying "dreams are visions of another dimension where things work differently, for why else would we have them?"

We have various regions of the brain that, when stimulated, allow us to guess their function- the stimulation of one region may cause involuntary muscle contractions, while others may elicit different emotions and mental states. While the "true" reason for why we have such a reaction is up to neurologists to argue about, I would not be surprised if it were merely some regions that were responsible for emotions such as "awe/wonder" or the "importance of things" that were going into overdrive when stimulated. This is mere speculation on my part, but this is more plausible than there being some supernatural force which they detect. Also involved might be some region that allows us to distinguish between ourselves and everything else: when I was deeply into Buddhism, I was able to sometimes induce this state in myself, where everything was almost as a dream and I seemed not just an individual but "part of everything." Participants in some studies who have had their brains stimulated describe similar experiences.

In any case, the question should be what evolutionary purpose such a mechanism serves, or if it indeed does have a concrete function or appears merely as an unintended consequence, or if it serves some more mundane role, such as the feeling of "wonder," and only when overstimulated gives way to a sense that "wow, I know the meaning of the universe!!" Those are the questions we should be asking — not "so therefore God exists?"

Argument from personal experience

> Gram: So what is your reason for believing that the Christian god is the correct one — why not Allah or Vishnu?

> Jim: I have had it revealed to me in such a way that I know it is true.

There is no easy way to disprove a "personal experience," and if a person says that they have had such an experience, I have no problem accepting that they believe in what they are saying. However, when such a claim arises, instead of just accepting that ("Wow! They had a personal experience! It must be true!"), you can inquire into what sort of experience it was, and how they are sure it was actually a god and not their brain fooling them in some way. However, chances are that the reply will be very vague: that they just "know."

If they "just know," point out that you "don't just know" since that is an unreliable way of knowing, and that plenty of people know different — other people may "just know" that Hinduism is the correct worldview or that fairies are real.

Other times, however, you might get a more concrete answer such as "God spoke to me." Whenever you get an unprovable personal account, point out that there are plenty of people who claim to have been visited by aliens — should you believe them all as well?

If the theist answers "yes — believe all of those accounts," then point out that that will mean that you will have to believe everything everyone tells you — from abductions to personal accounts from different contradictory religions, so that would be untenable.

Everyone has a right to believe anything they want. Although, when it comes to convincing somebody with even a miniscule amount of training in critical thinking, then a personal account, no matter how vivid and emotional, simply won't do the trick. If a god could land somewhere where a group of scientists could observe it and take samples — now that would be a step in the right direction.

Dialog 1

Jim: I have had it revealed to me in such a way that I know it is true.

Gram: May I ask, if not a secret, in what way was it revealed to you?

Jim: I just had this sudden realization, and "knew" that God was real.

Gram: It is your right to believe anything you want, however when it comes to convincing others of your beliefs, do you see how that might not be sufficient?

Dialog 2

Mary: I've been a total atheist, but then I was walking down this street at sunset, right after losing my mother, and suddenly I fell, and this deep thundering voice told me: " Mary, I am Jehovah your God — live life to the fullest and perform good deeds in my name! Your mother is waiting and she will be very proud!" When I stood up, I had complete faith from then on.

Samantha: That sounds like an epic experience — you heard God, and he said wondrous things... (empathy)

Mary: Indeed, it was the defining moment of my life.

Samantha: However could it have been something else —a hallucination perhaps? After all, you just lost your mother and also you fell.

Mary: No, I am sure it was God.

Samantha: But people with delusions are also sure about their delusions — that's what makes them delusional. If you were born in another culture, would you not have had appropriate visions from that culture?

Mary: NO! There is no way — the experience was too real.

Samantha: The problem is, how do we tell them apart — there are people you can talk to who will claim that they were abducted by aliens, not to mention people with divine experiences from different religions. How would you be able to differentiate their experiences from delusions?

Mary: Why do you insist on questioning my experience? It gives meaning to my life. What sort of insensitive person would do such a thing? (appeal to shame)

Samantha: I'm sure it was, but that doesn't answer my question. If I were to claim that I was abducted by aliens, surely you wouldn't just accept that at face value. Attempting to shame someone for questioning your beliefs when you do not have a good reply is disingenuous. Goodbye.

That last conversation did not end so well in terms of cordiality, but Mary will remember that she didn't have a good reply, and maybe, just maybe, do some actual thinking. Being polite and avoiding the most sensitive issues is not the proper tactic to take, as it would just validate the believer in thinking that everyone either agrees with him or has no good counter-argument to present. Of course, the discussion could have gone either way and Samantha could have agreed that there was no way to discern her experience from a delusion, and so the discussion could have ended on that cordial note.

If you make a theist uncomfortable by giving provocative questions, that is actually very good, since that means you are actually getting somewhere. Society teaches us from birth that it is improper to make other people uncomfortable — that that is bad manners. However, here it means that you are getting somewhere. No pain = no gain for the theist.

Transcendental argument for the existence of God (TAG)

The transcendental argument states that the universe has logical absolutes (for instance, something cannot be both true and false at the same time, and in the same sense), that logical absolutes are not part of the material world (they are conceptual), so require a mind to "host" them, and that mind of course is the mind of God. Without God, it would be impossible to think rationally since there would be no logic, which God created. Here is the short version:

1. The universe contains logical absolutes, math, etc.

2. Those things are conceptual — they require a mind to exist.

3. The mind is that of God.

This argument is often presented with a lot of excess points and a lot of verbiage, but the above paragraph sums it up nicely. You are highly unlikely to hear this argument from an average believer, and chances are if you are hearing it, you are being proselytized to. Ask if this argument, which the believer is presenting to you, is the true reason for that person's faith, or if it is just a card trick.

Dismantling the transcendental argument is fairly straightforward, but expect a lot of resistance from the believer and attempts at obfuscation: the Achille's heel of TAG is that it conflates conceptual statements (for instance, 2 is equal to 2) with how that relates to the real world. Logic, Mathematics and reason are not some divine things that are written somewhere on some magical rulebook of the universe, that, if one were to change, would make the world behave differently, but are "tools" created by humanity to better understand and describe the universe. As such, they can be compared to language: if English were to disappear, for instance, all of the things that are described in it, like cats and dogs, would not disappear as well because there is suddenly no word for them. In the same way, the underlying phenomena of a rock lying by itself, and another rock falling nearby, resulting in two rocks, would not disappear due to there being no one to keep track of said rocks or to create mathematical formulas. No one would describe it, and it would just be one large grouping of rock material next to another a short distance away — describing them as separate entities and counting them is a human activity.

Towards the end, you might also be presented with the notion that a god is somehow required for rational thought. Reasoning skills, however, are mental tools that humans use to understand the world, and require no outer source other than perhaps a good education and some books on skepticism and critical thinking.

> Mark: So, the universe contains logic — for instance one plus one is always two, and two is always equal to two. Do you agree?

> Jill: I don't think this is "contained" anywhere as rules, but rather that we use logic and reason do describe reality. You're confusing logical statements and what they are used to describe in the real world.

> Mark: But see, you said "logical statements" — where do they originate from?

> Jill: Just like language, they are created by humans to help them to describe the world and solve problems.

Using obscure scientific or mathematical notions such as quantum mechanics or the principle of infinity to prove the existence of the soul/God

The Internet is full of articles such as "A pair of world-renowned quantum scientists say they can prove the existence of the soul." or "Scientists Claim Quantum Theory Proves Consciousness Moves to Another Universe at Death." I could, if I was as smart as Stephen Hawking, write an entire book that refuted every such article. However, the good news is that you don't need to understand quantum mechanics, advanced mathematical principles or anything else sciency to be able to easily refute these claims. Often, the believer will speak of references to such research or articles. It is worth looking at the types of websites that usually host these articles: at best, they are popular magazines merely looking to attract readers, at worst there are some "faith-based" websites that clearly have an agenda. Luckily, it is the burden of those very scientists who have published these results to actually have them peer-reviewed - a process where other scientists look at their findings and try their best to show them why they are wrong. Only if those scientists cannot discredit them, and their results are reproducible (the scientists doing the testing come up with the same results) will this become a widely accepted scientific notion and not a "fringe idea." If we start seeing such articles pop up in scientific journals and magazines — then we are getting somewhere, since those magazines have their reputation at stake.

If during your discussion about religion you hear anything that includes words such as "quantum flux," "energy fields," "wave-particle duality," or anything else that sounds "sciency," it is most likely that the person in question is using these terms incorrectly — the only exception being if you are actually talking to a quantum physicist.

Usually the "logic" of such people is as follows:
1. I want God, souls, or an afterlife to exist.
2. I don't understand science or quantum mechanics very well (or at all).
3. There is some concept in quantum mechanics that sounds vaguely like something that proves a god — so it must be that!

If you hear such jargon, do not feign knowledge — ask about these concepts and about that they mean. It is most probable that your interlocutor won't be able to provide you with a coherent explanation and instead will spew out more jargon, poetry and analogies.

> **YOU DO NOT NEED TO BE A QUANTUM PHYSICIST TO REFUTE SUCH CLAIMS!**

Yes, the above really did need to be all-capitalized, because I couldn't overstress this point enough. You don't need to understand quantum mechanics or any such advanced scientific concept that is thrown against you — rather, all you have to do is point out that your interlocutor most likely does not have a degree in that subject either, and even if he does then it still won't matter, since the other people from that field do not share his opinions.[1] Prior to quantum mechanics, radiation was the hip esoteric sciency thing, and was used for "rejuvenation" in things such as creams and lipsticks.

Example dialogue:

Josh: For one thing, look at the advances made in quantum mechanics — the wave-particle duality, for one, which shows that the universe "knows" that you're looking at it, because, depending if there is an observer or not, the light behaves either as particles or

[1] There is no reputable science in which the consensus is that a certain theory or finding "proves" God's existence, or anything supernatural. At best there are fringe scientists who want to sell "sciency" books or appear on T.V.

as waves — if the universe knows that someone is watching, who is it that knows? It can only be God.

Millard: That is indeed an interesting experiment, and I do not claim to have advanced knowledge of quantum mechanics — however why is it that the vast majority of quantum theory scientists have not come to the same conclusion?

Josh: Well, they are just too analytical, too close-minded, I think, to have this sort of realization.

Millard: But they have spent years, probably decades studying these things, and here you come in, without any real knowledge of the subject, and after hearing some vague things about it, you claim that what they are studying proves your God — I think that this, instead, is the definition of arrogance and close-mindedness.

Defining God into existence

Some people play with definitions to get where they want to go. Examples:

God is reality.

God is perfection — reality is perfect, therefore God exists.

God is love.

God is the universe.

This is word play, pure and simple. What's being done is that a term that we know already exists, such as "love," is taken, and God is being equated to that term, so that if you believe in love, then you are actually not an atheist! Voilà!

However, equating God to a word that already has a definition, like "the universe," makes the God term redundant — we already have a word for the universe, so why use God? The answer is quite clear — it is a Trojan horse that tries to add more implications and meaning than we associate with those words: a God is usually seen as a conscious, all-knowing, all-powerful being, and we did not agree with the theist that the universe contains or consists of such an entity.

If the theist argues that no such a heist is afoot, then propose these counterexamples:

God is my smart phone.

God is the lunch I ate yesterday, and is limited to that lunch and nothing more.

God is my pet cat.

After all, if the theist can randomly pick words out of the dictionary and equate them with God, shouldn't you be allowed the same privilege?

Example dialogue:

> Jill: I actually think that you already believe in God, you just don't know it yet.

> Ryan: Well, first off, what do you mean by God — which one in particular?

> Jill: I'm a pantheist, so to me, God and the Universe are one and the same.

> Ryan: Okay, but we already have a word for the universe, it's "the universe" — why use God?

Ad hoc rationalizations

> *"Yes, but the communion wafer turns into the flesh of Christ when it is already in your mouth, which is why if you examine it with a microscope, you think it's just a wafer."*

In more colloquial terms, this is simply "making excuses" when your beliefs are questioned. They are not "real explanations" and are but Band-Aids for the believer's sinking ship of faith. If you feel that you have already countered a believer's argument and he begins coming up with nonsensical excuses, be sure to point it out and do not play into that "game." For instance, in the above communion wafer example, do you think the believer would have been sympathetic to the idea of testing his ad hoc rationalization by vomiting the wafer out, or spitting it out, and then testing it in a lab?

A model response to this type of behavior would be a line like "look, you are making excuses, and are not applying this skepticism equally to yourself — I can play that game, too, if you want (provide examples of similarly dishonest counter claims). Instead of doing that, how about you do some research, and if you can up with something real, then we can talk?"

Examples:

Dialog 1

Orson: There is an alien living in my kitchen!

Bob: Really? Can I see him?

Orson: No, he is very shy and will hide.

Bob: Perhaps you could record him on video?

Orson: No, due to his chemical composition, he would not be visible to the camera.

Bob: What if I have a look while he is asleep?

Orson: No, aliens don't sleep.

Bob: Can I look at him through binoculars from outside?

Orson: No, he has great eyesight and radar-vision; he will detect you from miles away.

Dialog 2

Luke: I believe that there is a teapot in orbit around the sun in our solar system.

Jane: Could we find it using a telescope?

Luke: No, it is invisible.

Jane: Perhaps then, we could track it via radar.

Luke: No, this teapot is transcendental and radio beams just pass through it.

Jane: That's OK! I have meditated long and hard, and have the ability to detect teapots with my mind!

Luke: Now you're just making fun.

Jane: I'm giving you a taste of your own medicine — if you have the right to come up with rationalizations, then the gloves are off and I have the same right.

— This dialogue is based on the idea of Russell's teapot (by Bertrand Russell, 1872–1970)

Exercise time!

Name the logical fallacies and "tricks" used in the sentences below:
1. Well, we have math and reason, and those things are necessarily contingent upon a mind — the mind would necessarily be infinitely complex, and could only be that of God.
2. I think that you believe in God as well — after all, you believe in Love, correct?
3. I just "know" God exists — I can feel it, as if it were a sense.
4. Don't you know that in Wiseman's 3:15 it says, "And ye, skeptics, repent! For surely thou are misguided and feeble minded!"
5. But without God, there can be no meaning in one's life.

"Scientists discovered the 'God Particle,' so how can God not exist then?"

The "God Particle" refers to the Higgs boson. A boson is a class of particles in quantum mechanics (there are two of them — bosons and fermions). The Higgs boson was theorized in 1964 and was finally shown to exist only recently using the Large Hadron Collider at CERN. What the discovery boils down to is that we now have a better understanding of why some fundamental particles have mass. If you'd like to go on examining the intricacies of this discovery you can read about it on Wikipedia.[1] In short, all that this discovery reveals is "why some particles have mass." No mention of any divine being or cosmic intelligence — none of the sort. Indeed, the term "God Particle" is strongly disliked by physicists, including Peter Higgs, whom this particle is named after. In essence, we have an important scientific discovery that then got sensationalized and re-branded in the mainstream media, completely distorting the point of the original discovery.

The term "God Particle" was coined by physicist Leon Lederman, who used it in a book of the same name. Why would a physicist use such a term? Because according to him it so crucial in understanding the universe, yet so very difficult to observe. Get it? The term, in its own way, was actually meant to poke fun at religion, not lend any credence to it.

Example dialogue:

> Mike: Scientists discovered the "God Particle," so how can God not exist then?
>
> Jane: Do you know what it actually is though?
>
> Mike: I think it's called the Higgs boson...
>
> Jane: Yes, and what is that? What are the implications of knowing that the Higgs boson exists?

[1]http://en.wikipedia.org/wiki/Higgs_boson

Mike: That God exists?

Jane: No, it has nothing to do with God — this discovery helps us better understand why some fundamental particles have mass. Do you know why it was called the "God Particle?"

Mike: Why?

Jane: Well, it was coined by a physicist because according to him that particle was so crucial in understanding the universe, yet so elusive and difficult to detect, like God. He was actually poking fun at religion, in his own small way.

"My religion is the only one in which _____."

Each religion has its own claim to fame — indeed, they can have many. Jews have the (Hebrew-speaking) Burning Bush, Christianity has the "man who rose from the dead" (Mormonism in fact has two such men), Islam has "the linguistic miracle of the Quran" and so forth. The problem is that those are all just that — claims. Its equivalent to arguing about superheroes from comic books: each superhero has his unique power, albeit fictional.

"Some of the places/events in my holy book have been found out to be real — therefore my religion is the correct one!"

Here, we may again use the comic book analogy. A great example, coined by Russell Glasser of the *Atheist Experience*, is that by this logic, if thousands of years from now archeologists discover a Spider-Man comic book, and then find the ruins of New York where some of the events took place, then they would conclude that Spider-Man had truly existed. This is of course not how historians operate; the mere existence of a location that was mentioned in a story doesn't validate the actual story. What would lend more credibilty to the story is if other second-hand accounts of it existed from official records or passers-by. This is how we know, for instance, that Muhammad existed — his existence is not in question since he had dealings with outsiders who recorded their interactions, not to mention that he left descendants. His more "miraculous" deeds, however, like those of any other miracle worker, lack that kind of documentary back-up. When it comes to resurrection, you'd think that both every literate person in town would have been sufficiently impressed with that so as to have written something down — alas, we have no such records except for the Bible.

Presuppositional apologetics

Dealing with presuppositional apologetics is especially arduous: the whole notion of "pre-supposing that they are already correct" sort of puts a damper on any hope of progress.

The three presuppositions that Christian presuppositionalists commonly hold are:

1. The Christian God Exists.
2. The Bible is revealed knowledge of that God.
3. The Sense of the "Holy Spirit."

The core notion goes like this: it is impossible to reason rationally without God (particularly, the God that the apologist believes in) since God is the source of reason. How does he/she know that God exists? Because it "has been revealed to him/her." Any argument you present will be seen through the lens of the Bible/Quran being inerrant, or through God having to exist. Presuppositional apologists often attack reason, rationality and science, claiming that their use is just as circular as using the Bible to confirm God (why this is not the case was discussed at the beginning of this chapter).

When dealing with presuppositional apologetics it is important to understand the apologist's position:

Reason/Logic/Rationality is contingent upon God

When being presented with this apologetic, it is useful to inquire about which god in particular it is contingent upon, and if any evidence exists for such a god.

Properly Basic Beliefs — Much as we like to think that we can come up with logical explanations for everything, we are still forced to use certain core beliefs which we cannot justify, such as "I exist" and that "logic/reason works." Much as you'd want to justify why reason is a good thing, you'd only be using reason to do so, which is circular. Do not fall into the trap of trying to defend reason by using reason: presuppositionalists sometimes give this impossible to fulfill task, which neither you nor the presuppositionalists themselves can fulfill, since you will be reasoning to reach your conclusion. Even if you are tempted to scream out, "I use reason because it works!" — ask yourself, how exactly did you come to that conclusion? Chances are, you reasoned into it. Apologists will try to sneak "The belief in God" as a properly basic belief — and this is where you catch them: A belief in God is by no means properly basic — first off, large numbers of people don't believe in God, whereas you'd be hard-pressed to find individuals who don't believe that they exist,[1] furthermore, apologetics requires reasoning — let me repeat that:

The belief in God is contingent upon other presuppositions.

If a belief is built upon other beliefs, then it is not properly basic. First off, the two presuppositions listed above will be useless without the use of the other properly basic beliefs such as knowing that you exist and that

---

[1] Some faiths, including Buddhism, teach that this reality is all an illusion, however even the most ardent Buddhists would have to acknowledge that within this "illusion" they still have bodies and minds.

reasoning is possible — without those, any sort of intellectual discourse is impossible. (They may try to deny that it is reason — but this denial is once again the use of reason.) Furthermore, when it comes to the notion that "The Bible is the Inspired word of God" — to even begin to contemplate that, you must already presuppose that the world is not merely your imagination (a mind-independent reality) since the Bible is a physical book that is part of that world, and that other minds exist — those that were inspired by God to write the Bible, as well as that God himself exists. Even when it comes to "The sense of the holy spirit" — that requires the presupposition of other minds, and that you exist.

The good thing in holding these properly basic beliefs (such as: "reason works" and that other people are conscious, just like us), is that they allow us to have a better grounding in reality. Having these beliefs stops us from asserting, "Well, there all of those properly basic beliefs, surely this belief that I really treasure is a properly basic belief," but it also allows us to decide that some other beliefs are just plain unfounded. Belief in the divine is no more a basic belief than that of aliens, string theory, the Greek pantheon or republicanism.

One must use Occam's razor to not multiply explanatory entities beyond what is strictly necessary to explain something. Explanations must only be as complicated as they need to be to explain something. If a premise holds no explanatory power, such as "demons are responsible for bad weather," then it is useless. Belief in gods is just as useless, since there are ideas that explain more clearly the things gods are supposed to explain, like how the universe originated, weather events, sickness, and what happens after we die. Believing in gods will not give you any useful insight into how the world works — you cannot "test God."[1]

Neither does it matter if a belief is internally-consistent, something that apologists often claim about Christianity.[2] A belief can be internally consistent but still not correspond to reality. Internal consistency does not mean that something is true. In fact, many of today's scientific ideas have inconsistencies — but that does not mean we should throw them all out, all it means is that we have to keep on digging till we clear everything up.

If you want "proof" of something, you argument has to be:
- Formally valid — the rules of logic are properly applied.
- The premises must be true.

For example, the following syllogism is valid since both the logic and premises are true:

All men are mortal.

Socrates is a man.

Therefore, Socrates is mortal.

[1] Or indeed, all of our attempts thus far have shown that no Gods exist.
[2] And Christianity is by no means internally consistent — Google "Contradictions in the Bible."

In this one, however, I tweaked the premises a bit:

All men are Asian.

Socrates is a man.

Therefore, Socrates is Asian.

This argument is logically valid; however, it is not "sound" — for that, both the logic and premises must be true.

In this final syllogism the logic is not valid — this is pretty common among theists:

All men are mortal.

Socrates is a man.

Therefore God exists!

The presuppositions that Christian apologists use are not "true presuppositions," in the sense of "properly basic beliefs" — rather, they are merely disguised theological dogmas that they attempt to slip in like a Trojan horse. To exist they require a multitude of "true" properly basic beliefs, and offer nothing useful in return — they are parasitic in nature. Call them out on it.

An analogy:

If you still aren't getting through, it's time to use an analogy with fluffy bunnies!

Long, long ago, far, far away, there existed some cute bunny rabbits aboard a spaceship. Their presupposition was:

> "There exists a giant computer somewhere in the universe that makes us rabbit-like."

However, this again is "dogma" masquerading as a properly-basic belief: to be able to understand the above sentence rabbits must at the very least agree with the presupposition that "there is a reality within which that can occur," also that "reason works" — since computers function through logic, and that other rabbits with distinct minds exist which can also be made "rabbit-like." Furthermore, the rabbits have no evidence of that computer's existence — it was passed on to them through the tales of the ancients. There is a sacred screw, however, that is said to be from a cooling duct that cooled the circuitry of that computer, is known about and worshipped inside a giant black cube that able rabbits must visit at least once in their lives, called the "Raaba" — however, that won't convince any non-rabbits.

The presuppositionalist "routine" in a nutshell, and how to exit it. I will be using the term "presup" instead of presuppositionalist since it sounds more street.

Presup: How do you know X?

Newbie: I used reason/evidence to come to the conclusion that X!

Presup: How do you know reason and evidence is reliable?! This could all be an illusion!

Newbie: I used reason because it works!

Presup: Aha! You are using reason to prove reason. Your argument is circular!

(The newbie counter-apologist attempted to "prove" reason — this is what the presup wants.)

Presup: How do you know reason and evidence is reliable?! This could all be an illusion!

Skeptic: Why, sir, indeed I do not know — we could be "brains in vats" or "in the Matrix" — do YOU know? And if so, then how?

Presup: Why, yes, I do, and it is through the Bible! It is the truth (alternatively, the truth could be "revealed" to the presup, or it could be faith or a divine sense).

Skeptic: And how do you know that THAT is reliable!?

Presup: The Bible tells me so! (Alternatively, faith proves faith or it is "revealed")

Now that you have this "hook," go on the offensive — explain why faith or divine revelation isn't reliable and do not allow your presup to go back to the same arguments twice — use a graceful exit for that.

Use the phrase "your premise is unfounded!" as often as possible.[1]

Finally, here are the "tenets" one must have when dealing with a presup:
1. Do not attempt to use reason to justify reason.
2. You "do not know" if a god does exist.
3. You "do not know" if we are all "in the Matrix/brains in vats."
4. The presup doesn't "know" either; he only "pretends to know things he doesn't know" (has faith).
5. The burden of proof is on the presup to demonstrate that a god does exit or that the logical absolutes are contingent upon the presups' god.
6. The belief in God is not a properly-basic belief.

For examples of a debate with a presuppositional apologist, search YouTube for:
"Matt Slick vs. Matt Dillahunty"
"Matt Dillahunty vs. Sye Ten Bruggencate"
Presuppositionalists often employ the "Transcendental Argument for the Existence of God" which was described previously.

---

[1] Credit goes to the awesome "Russell Glasser" from "The Atheist Experience" for that phrase.

God exists, because without him life would be meaningless.

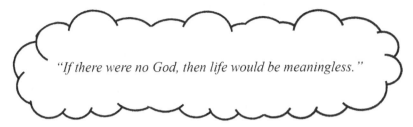

"*If there were no God, then life would be meaningless.*"

It is hard to even call this argument an argument for the existence of a god, since it only deals with the emotional repercussions — for instance, "If there are no aliens... then space exploration would be meaningless." This argument relies on the notion that there is a single absolute meaning of life carved somewhere on the fabric of the universe. Of course, here on Earth, even if there were no atheists, it would still be subjective because of the sheer amount of people and religions. The theist's "absolute meaning" is still subjective; while he thinks that it is absolute, that is just his subjective opinion. On the other hand, we atheists can stick to the motto, "The meaning of one's life is to give meaning to one's life." It is not up to someone else to choose our passions in life, what lines of knowledge to pursue, and how to spend our time — it is all on us. Even religious believers are wary of government "dictating" or interfering in their personal decisions; but suddenly, if it's an omnipotent being, that would be OK? I think not.

This argument is often a diversion from the real discussion of whether or not a god actually exists. Usually this argument is employed later on in the discussion, when you began to question the faith of the believer.

Exercise Time! (Counter-Apologetics Part 3)

Think up a brief response:
1. The president believes in God!
2. The discovery of the God particle proves God!
3. Everything that begins to exist must have a cause. The universe began to exist. The universe must therefore have a cause. That cause is God.
4. I think that you believe in God as well — after all, you believe in Love, right?
5. The universe contains the laws of logic. These laws require a mind. The mind can only be that of God.
6. But don't you wish you would be able to see your family in heaven after you die?
7. I just "know" God exists — as if it were a sense.

Talking to Believers

You and the believer

It's best to place yourself in the mindset of "therapist" and "patient" as opposed to "atheist" and "theist." This is done with a concrete purpose — not to convey the message that all believers are somehow insane, but rather to shift the model of discussion from "debate" to "therapy/intervention." Words carry hidden baggage with them — this is why many successful companies tend to replace traditional terms with fancy terms such as Barista (Starbucks), which gives it a more upper class feel, and the term "actor" (Disney Land) is used for everyone who is "on stage" (outside, interacting with the visitors). Even janitors are "actors" since it breaks the traditional notion that a janitor, say, may simply clean the floor, fix things and ignore everything else, but rather, if he is an "actor" then he should also act friendly and cheerfully towards the visitors and not break the spell of their visit. [1]

In the same way, the terms "theist" and "atheist" carry with them cultural preconceptions about how discussions should go:

Theists and atheists are seen as "debaters" — both proclaim their arguments and try to convince the other.

Patients and therapists have a "healer–patient" structure, where one person tries to help the other overcome a malady.

You can develop the mindset of helping the other person recover — he is the victim of a delusion, and calling him stupid won't help. By mentally labeling yourself as a "therapist," I hope you can instill these values in yourself:

- Compassion
- Resoluteness
- Do No Harm

By contrast, being in "Debater" mode, you might feel driven to:

- Show that "You" are correct.
- Show that the "Opponent" is wrong.
- Take pride in your argument.

These do not require further explanation. Reading this book won't make you a therapist, but it may help you see yourself in the social role of a "healer" instead of "a debater." You are not there to debate — you are there to tear away the patient's delusions at their core with a swift, precise slice of the knife of skepticism, and to comfort them afterwards. Unless, of course, you are being ganged up on by believers or in harassed in any way — in that case you need a different approach. You are not obligated to debate and can simply walk away.

---

[1] For more, read *Made to Stick: Why Some Ideas Survive and Others Die*, by brothers Chip and Dan Heath.

Do not use jargon

Consider these two sentences:

1. "Ahh, you've committed the argument from ignorance followed by the argument from authority — these are both logical fallacies, plus the burden of proof is on you!"
2. "Well, simply because you can't imagine another way for something to occur, that doesn't automatically make your idea the correct one. Even if many people believe something, that doesn't automatically make it true. If you make a claim, it is up to you to provide the evidence if you want me to believe it."

While the first one is shorter, if a person has not read up on critical thinking and skepticism, it will probably make his eyes glaze over. Imagine you were speaking to either an elderly person or a five-year-old — how would you explain things to them? Simply, concisely and to the point, and without being snide. You can save the jargon for your atheist friends.

This is not condescension — to engage with someone, you have to "meet them where they are." Imagine that you are a real-life astronaut, and you have to talk to some non-scientist people. Rather than give the impression that you don't even care if they understand what you're saying, you want to engage with said people and show them how exciting your world, your profession, is: seeing the earth from orbit, the experience of zero gravity, etc. The same goes for any other type of discussion where one person wants to convey an idea. For more, I'd recommend *Made to Stick: Why Some Ideas Survive and Others Die* by Chip Health.

Empathy is important! Don't talk past each other.

When a theist professes some viewpoint, instead of countering it, it is important to showcase that you understand what he or she is saying and are not just waiting with a comeback response. Instead, when a theist professes something, repeat it in your own words, before countering it. This will show that you are "really listening."

• Before going "on the offensive," it is useful to have a "map" of the theist's beliefs, otherwise you are just going in blind — let the theist talk, and truly listen and try to understand where he or she is coming from.

• A cookie-cutter way of talking is of no value to anyone — each discussion will have its particular nuances, however by learning the techniques and arguments in this book you will be in a stronger position.

• Don't be preachy!

• Don't assume that the believer's mind is a bucket, waiting to be filled up with the waters of knowledge. In reality, it's more like a fortress that lets in things that it recognizes.

• Instead of giving the person the conclusion, slowly guide him towards it — people accept ideas more readily if they think they came to them by themselves.

Let's have a look at these two example discussion styles:

Discussion1:

> Sam: I just believe in God, you know...

> Luke: Which one? There is no evidence for any religion that passes scrutiny.

> Sam: Right, but it gives me hope.

> Luke: You can get hope from other things: humanity, the beauty of nature.

> Sam: But that's not enough — all this is meaningless without God and faith.

> Luke: Faith is gullibility — you must learn to be more skeptical, otherwise you could believe anything.

> Sam: My faith keeps me strong.

Discussion 2:

> Sam: I just believe in God, you know...

> Luke: Which one in particular? There are many different notions of gods among different cultures.

> Sam: The Christian god.

> Luke: Interesting — may I ask, how do you know God exists?

> Sam: You just got to have faith.

> Luke: But say a Muslim person or a Hindu approached you with their notions and their faith, how would you show them that your notion of God is the correct one?

> Sam: I'd show them the Biblical proof.

> Luke: So it seems to me that you initially said you used faith, but then you switched to using Biblical proof — perhaps you should look up the history of the different faiths of the world, and that way you could have a more solid answer and come back to me sometime later so we can continue this discussion?

Sam: Sure, I'll get back to you.

Which one of these discussions seems to be the most productive? I'd wager it was the second one. Why?

What the atheist in the first discussion did WRONG:

1. He used Prescriptive Language, that is, he told the believer what to think — as in "you must," "you shouldn't," "what you should do is..." — people don't respond well to such commands.

Atheist: "faith is gullibility — you must learn to be more skeptical, otherwise you could believe anything."

2. He used closed answers — instead of leading the person onwards and making him think for himself, in many an instance he said the equivalent of "you are wrong — here is the correct answer ____."

Atheist: "Which one? There is no evidence for any religion that passes scrutiny."

This lead to a "yes, but..." feedback from the believer; here is a simplified example:

Mark: That show is so annoying.

Lilly: You could switch channels.

Mark: Yes, but I doubt there is anything better on.

Lilly: You could try the news.

Mark: Yes, but I've already seen the news this morning.

Lilly: You could turn off the TV.

Mark: Yes, but I'm too tired to do anything else right now.

To get out of such a loop without killing your interlocutor, there are two very nice strategies:

1. Suggest several options: "Well, we could go out, switch channels or eat." — When presented with different choices, it's much harder to say "No, I will not do any of that."

2. Ask your interlocutor what he'd prefer to do, instead of offering choices.

What the atheist in Discussion 2 did CORRECTLY:

He did not shut the believer down as soon as she told him about her beliefs — instead he clarified what exactly she believes in. In "The Atheist Experience" show, there is a standard question that the hosts use when a theist calls in, which is, "What do you believe in and why?"[1] "God" is an ambiguous term that requires pinning down — don't let your interlocutors get away with sneaking through a vague notion of god.

If they do end up with a vague definition, it's best to make them acknowledge said fact.

Atheist: "Which one in particular? There are many different notions of gods among different cultures."

2. Next, instead of using prescriptive language such as "There is no evidence for any god," he dived deeper into the person's reasoning to continue the discussion:

Atheist: "Interesting — may I ask, how do you know God exists?"

3. Finally, the "graceful exist" — instead of backing the person into a corner, the atheist asked the believer to "do more research" on how his faith is more valid than other faiths and how to differentiate between fact and fiction. When the ego is not at stake, people can unleash their full intellectual potential. Don't try to force people into changing their opinions on the spot — give them time to digest the new information and come back with a better answer.

Read up on *Motivational Interviewing* by William R. Miller and Stephen Rollnick — it's not about atheism and is meant for actual psychotherapists dealing with issues such as alcoholism and depression. The above "Discussion 2" was inspired by the techniques taught there, and this book is useful on its own as it can teach you how to be a more empathetic listener and "guide" instead of shoving advice down people's throats.

Do not appease dishonesty and avoidance.

Example Conversation:

Mark: You just got to have faith.

Lilly: But, say a Muslim person or a Hindu approached you with their notions and their faith, how would you show them that your notion of God is the correct one?

Mark: I have the faith to know.

---

[1] Another variant is, "What do you believe in and why do you believe in it?"

Lilly: Sure, but those also have their faiths — how can you discern which of those faiths is correct?

Mark: Through faith.

Lilly: I sense that you're uncomfortable discussing this and are simply repeating your answer. It's OK not to know — how about this: do some research on why your faith is the correct one and how you can tell, and then if you wish we can continue this discussion.

Analysis: in the above conversation the believer was actively using the "through faith" excuse even when its lack of validity was explained several times. When you get this barrier, do not switch topics, or get frustrated — instead, describe exactly what happened and then do the "Graceful Exit" — "How about you read up about this and we can talk later?" By agreeing to "read up," the believer timidly acknowledges that the lack of knowledge is on her part, not yours.

You are not obliged to read their scriptures!

To question my faith you must first read my holy book.
All of the questions you have are answered in my holy book.
My holy book proves my religion!
Fortunately, you are not required to read every holy book, although it helps on a personal level to understand these books, if for nothing more than closure — only after reading them will the nagging question "What if there is actually something super profound in one of those books?" be answered. With me it was a resounding "no" — my thoughts on these examples of human creativity can be found later in this book, but overall I found them at best amusing and at worst nonsensical, inhumane and badly-written. The only value of these books that I can find is seeing the mindset of people at the time in which they were written — if even a badly skewed one, since prophets are not always on the same wavelength as regular folk.

While reading is beneficial, it will likely not be the deciding factor. Here are some responses that you may get upon revealing that you have indeed read the holy book, and find it unimpressive:

1. You must read it again — clearly you didn't understand it!

2. You must have more faith.

3. The misgivings you have are there because you read it in English and not in Ancient Mestrophaxis.

(Note: I made that up as an obscure language that no one except a few anthropologists or linguists could possibly be familiar with.)

If you find yourself in this situation, go this route:

Jake: To be able to question my faith, you must first read the Quran.

Fogul: Okay, I might just do that.

Jake: Good.

Fogul: Tell me, though, since I'm interested to know how you think — say for instance people were to approach me many times a day, bringing me large books that they claim contain wondrous writings and secrets of the universe, and each of those books would take years to fully understand, but I don't know in advance if any of them were the writings of madmen or geniuses, then how would I decide which ones I should read, if any?

Use parables and analogies if you notice you are going in circles.

In some of the previous examples, you saw dialogues where the atheist told a parable to demonstrate the error in thinking that the theist had committed. A parable will allow the theist to distance himself from his ego — after all, it is not "him" in the parable, and as such he will be able to observe the situation more objectively. Do not launch into a parable every second sentence — use them sparingly. If you use a parable or short story every time the theist commits a logical fallacy, you'll end up telling all of them, and you will be deemed annoying or condescending.

Using a parable to explain why the theist is wrong is not "rude" or "insulting."

Theists have been using parables for thousands of years. If someone quotes the Bible or another holy book at you, chances are it will be a parable. There is a reason for this — short stories with actual people in analogous situations "stick" in the mind far better than just a logical explanation of fact. In *Made to Stick*, Chip and Dan Heath gave the example of dividing a class of Stanford University students into small groups, and having them give one-minute speeches about whether nonviolent crime is a serious problem in the US or not, while others would listen. Since they were Stanford students, all of them gave very good speeches and were usually rated highly by the other students in terms of eloquence and persuasiveness. However, after a mandatory 10-minute distraction, the students were then asked to remember each speech. Shockingly, they could remember almost none of the actual content. Humans are inherently bad at remembering statistics and factoids. However, using short emotional stories that drive in the point works like magic, and the chances of it "sticking" in memory are an order of magnitude higher. This is because this is what humans initially evolved to remember. Imagine these two scenarios:

Hunter-Gatherer #1: The efficacy of group-based hunting tactics using elongated spears for hunting megafauna is decreased proportionally with the decrease in temperature.

Hunter-Gatherer #2: Our group has lost many brave warriors during this last winter season: the giant beasts are harder to catch, and the cold bites our fingers and makes our spears harder to throw; so we're starving.

Which of those hunter gatherers would have been able to actually communicate his message? Unfortunately, while the harsh pre-historic period would have filtered out all of those ineffective speakers, in modern times there is a huge resurgence of jargon-based, indirect, abstract speech. Avoid it at all costs.

Do not "agree to disagree"

At the end of a discussion, the believer may use this phrase to amiably end the discussion. It may seem like the polite, reasonable and diplomatic thing to do. Agreeing to disagree, however, will legitimize his argument in his mind, since if no conclusion was reached, it would seem that both ideas are on equal footing.

John: Let's just agree to disagree.

Luke: Well, I can't do that.

John: (some surprised phrase)

Luke: (Reiterate your previous point, and "Gracefully Exit.")

Theist: Let's just agree to disagree.

Sage: You know, this reminds me of this one time I was in grade school.

Theist: Oh? Haha...

Sage: Yeah, it was one of those schools where two students share a desk. We were both solving a math problem, and I was sure the answer was 77. He was sure it was 79. We argued for a bit and then politely decided to agree to disagree — so we both decided to be diplomatic, and put 78 — that is, the "middle ground," as an answer. However, when we got back our results it turned out that his answer — 79, was the correct one.

Theist: Well, this is different — God is not a math's problem that can be analyzed through logic — you have to feel him in your soul and in everything else around you.

Sage: It depends — if we're talking about a god that created the universe and left the moment the Big Bang occurred, then sure. However, if we're talking about a god that responds to prayer and performs miracles, then no — since those are all testable claims that can either be shown to be correct or falsified.

Keep your discussions short

This may seem counterintuitive, since it looks as if the theist has so many misconceptions and knowledge gaps that need to be filled. However, you can hardly fill in the person's knowledge gaps in many or most of these areas:
1. Skepticism/ critical thinking
2. The scientific method
3. Basic biology
4. History
5. Origins of the universe
6. Origins of the earth
7. The flaws in their holy book
8. Comparative religion
9. Evolution

Your job is not to fill their jugs of knowledge — it is to burst their balloons of faith.

You don't need to grow their tree of skepticism — you just need to plant their seeds of doubt.

Chances are, if a discussion has been going on for hours, instead of "imparting knowledge" what has been happening is that you have been going around in circles, with the theist repeatedly bringing up the same argument after a suitable amount of time. If you notice that this is happening, it's best to point this out to the theist, and to do the graceful exit.

Be like an assassin — your mission is to get into Fort Delusion, snip the jugular of General Faith, and get out as soon as possible. The regime change will happen later on.

Keep on topic

If the theist notices that he is backed into an epistemological corner, he might attempt to sneakily change the subject — this takes some skill to detect and requires a firm resolve to point out and challenge. For instance, you might be discussing why faith is not a reliable way of knowing things, and all of a sudden you'll notice that the discussion has shifted away to the horrible imagined implications of the lack of faith in society. Do not allow the discussion to continue until the theist has acknowledged that faith is not a valid way of knowing things (which actually happens rarely in a discussion — usually, people finally agree to this after they have had some time to think).

Example dialogue:

Juan: ...And therefore pretending to know things that you don't know,[1] i.e., faith, is not a sound way to make decisions about what is real.

Martinez: But do you think society would not devolve into chaos without faith? What would most people do without morals? (Attempt to shift the discussion away to the presumed consequences of the lack of faith, and also to the origins of morality)

Juan: Hold on. I'm willing to have the discussion on those consequences, and where people get their morals from, but first do you acknowledge what I've said about faith not being a good way of knowing things?

Beware of topic-switching tactics

Apart from blatant topic-jumping, look out for the following phrases:
"Let's not get into that..."

"We could talk about it for days but..."

"That's a whole other rabbit hole..."

"That's not relevant..."

"That's not important..."

"Yeah, but that's out of context — let's talk about..."

If you notice the above phrases or phrases similar to them, instead of politely agreeing to avoid the issue, view those phrases as your opening. The reason that this topic-switching is occurring is that the religious person is now on the defensive. Do not allow them this retreat:

"Let's not get into that..."

Answer: Well, why not? I think we SHOULD talk about it; otherwise we will never get to the bottom of this issue.

"We could talk about it for days but..."

Answer: Very well, let's talk about it for days, since both you and I are interested in finding out the truth.

"That's not relevant..."

Answer: Well, I think it's completely relevant because _____.

"That's not important..."

Answer: Well, I think it's extremely important because _____.

"Yeah, but that's out of context — let's talk about..."

Answer: Wait, out of which context? Let's open up a Quran/Bible/

---

[1] Credit to *Peter Boghossian, "A Manual for Creating Atheists"* for that definition.

The Book of Mormon/ etc. and have look at the context. [1]

Of course, this is far from an exhaustive list — however, look out for this tactic (defense mechanism) in general.

Emotional retorts are not valid arguments

Have you ever had conversations where, upon more or less proving your point, the other person became emotional, abusive, or even worse — the "atomic bomb" — that is, crying?

> *Your father, brother and I will be very upset, devastated indeed, for the loss of your soul — just think of your granny — what would she think?*

This is just plain emotional manipulation. It's OK for your family and friends to be upset. You are not responsible for other people's feelings, and it is not your "responsibility" to pretend to be someone you are not just in order not to upset people. Imagine the same argument if you were gay: "Your granny and uncle would be so upset to find out that you are gay — how can you hurt everyone in this cruel fashion?," and you will instantly see where this argument goes wrong.

Apart from overt emotional reactions, the person may attempt to emotionally coerce you into "feeling bad for them." These are unfair debate tactics, like a kid throwing a tantrum, and should not be appeased, as then they would be taken as valid and used again. We will next take a look at two scenarios — this time the discussion will be between a husband and a wife, however keep in mind that you should still use the therapist/patient style of speech as much as possible in all such situations:

> Wife: After you told me that you're an atheist... I just don't know what will happen to your soul.

> Husband: Well, are you worried that I will go to the Islamic version of hell?

> Wife: What does that have to do with anything?

> Husband: Out of all the thousands of underworlds, you're only worried about one — you're not worried that my body won't be properly embalmed and put into a sarcophagus, so that by "ka" —

---

[1] As long as you have an Internet connection this should not be an issue — you can download an entire Bible/Quran/etc. in a matter of minutes, or look at any number of sites where the verses are available online.

the body double and "ba" — the personality, would be preserved — which is the only way that the ancient Egyptians thought they could reach an afterlife. Neither are you contemplating on putting a coin in my mouth if I were to die, which would pay for my way into Hades — the ancient Greek version. I could go on...

Wife: **turns away and begins crying**

Now, this is where one has to be decisive and not go the "appeasement" route of, "Honey I'm sorry" — instead:

Husband: I see you need some time to think this over; I'll be heading out to work now and we can talk again in a bit. I love you no matter what.

This type of firmness will show that you are not willing to break on this issue, and it is she who will have to decide how to proceed.

Other than overt emotional displays however, one might encounter subtler forms of emotional manipulation:

Mom: So you don't believe in any sort of afterlife?

Son: No, sorry, I don't: I realized that our religion is no more valid than all of the other countless faiths, and none of them have any evidence.

Mom: But... it makes me really sad that you won't be there with us up in heaven. Your parents will really miss you up there, hoping that you will change your mind — perhaps if you prayed, God would answer your prayers...

Depending on what you are going for, there are several ways to respond:

(1) Atheist: If you truly believe in a god that loves everybody, then you can pray for me, since that is the only way that I can be saved — you're not able to convince me with your arguments.

(2) Atheist: You're trying to emotionally coerce me into changing what I believe, and that is not how I'm going to change my mind — now, if you could provide something more valid then that would be great. Till then, please do more research into this area — especially try to research the difference between faith-based reasoning and critical thinking, and then maybe we can continue this discussion.

(3) Wisdom-Teller: You know, this reminds me of a story I once heard: In the 1570s, a little orphan girl kept telling everyone that her father was, in fact, the prince, and that one day he'd return and claim her. That story accomplished two things: it gave her hope, but it also made the other kids tease her. Whenever they would

tell her that her story was not true, she'd retort: "Don't you know it makes me really sad when you say that!" — And for a while the kids stopped. However, then she began issuing royal decrees and talking to people as if she were the queen and they were mere peasants — some kids even believed her and hoped for a good position later in life once her parents returned. Do you think this is a healthy way to live and perceive reality?

Being bombarded with religious verses

Do not allow yourself to be flooded. There is a particular type of theist that will constantly throw scripture at you. Cut this off at the very beginning. Remember the very first verse that you were given, and focus on that verse and how it relates to that person's faith. If it does not relate, then it is irrelevant to the discussion and you should tell them so. If, on the other hand, that verse is relevant, use that as a starting point to discuss why having faith in religious verses is not such a good idea — bring up the fact that other religions have them as well.

For these examples I'll use made up verses, to demonstrate that their content is of no relevance to the discussion.

Lurok: It says in WiseMan's 3:11 that "All humankind shalt worship the Benevolent One, the One that gives us life."

Bob: Okay, but that still didn't answer my question...

Lurok: Well, in Gutu's 32:1 it says "All shall be revealed, to those who ask."

Bob: Wait, let's get back to the first one — Wise-Man's was it?

Lurok: Yes, WiseMan's 3:11 that "All humankind shall worship the Benevolent One, the One that gives us life."

Bob: Okay, let's focus on this one for now.

Lurok: Ok?...

Bob: It must have been very important to you, for you to have brought it up?

Lurok: Yes... it's beautiful.

Bob: Am I correct in assuming that it is passages like these, among others, that give you your faith?

Lurok: yesss...

Bob: Okay, may I tell you my problem with this line of reasoning?

Lurok: *nods*

Bob: There are thousands of religions out there, and each has various beautiful verses, songs, and poems devoted to them — the problem is that, just as you have faith in these ones, other people believe in other verses which they think are beautiful that contradict yours... Using just verses, it is impossible to tell which, if any, are actually correct.

Lurok: Well, In Mahalo's 7:9 it says "Beware of doubt, it is of the fallen cities."

Bob: Okay, but right now we were talking about the virtue of passages in religious texts as a means of knowing, not of any individual passages.

Lurok: Well, the Book Of Good Virtue is supported by a tradition of accurate re-telling, and of historical evidence — hundreds of people have witnessed the Miracle of GruLz.

Bob: Well, people of other faiths, for example Islam, have even harder historical evidence, and there are people that you could talk to — today — that claim to have been abducted by UFOs — so if I had to allow for your standard of evidence, I'd have to let all those other claims in as well.

It's OK to criticize any culture or religion

This seems to be humanity's biggest taboo — it's fine to criticize politics, sports teams and cooking. But mention the most important topics of all: the questions "what happens after we die" and "how should we live our lives," and suddenly what you are doing is somehow incorrect. Indeed, this ban on the criticism of religion has no feet to stand on, and if you notice something that you think is incorrect, or downright harmful, then criticism of those things you deem wrong is the only intellectually, nay, morally acceptable decision.

Theist: You shouldn't criticize religions and cultures — it's socially unacceptable!

Atheist: You know what I consider socially unacceptable? Witch burnings, lashings, child marriage, stoning for leaving the faith and blasphemy, human sacrifice to prevent the end of the world — If we were all "polite" and "respectful," then these things would still be going on, and indeed some of them still are in some parts of the world. I say to hell with being respectful when important issues are at stake.

Theist: But those are all corrupt human interpretations of religion: God is love.

Atheist: Do you think the (Bible/Quran/whatever holy text) is accurate?

Theist: Yes!

Atheist: (points out various unloving parts of the book)

Theist: But that is taken out of context!

Atheist: Ok, let's have a look at the context (opens up the holy text and reads the text before and after the quote).

Atheist: Under which context is (slavery/genocide or something else we consider unacceptable that's mentioned in the text) acceptable? I say there should be no such context!

Theist: But that text is in the Old Testament — those rules no longer apply.

Atheist: But isn't God supposed to be omnipotent and all-knowing? Why would he make a society that would require different rules than we have today? I think you're just making excuses — because you yourself are more moral than that holy book, and you're searching desperately for excuses as to why that horrible stuff that was written there shouldn't be followed, and why it is no longer relevant.

There are plenty of online resources pointing out distasteful things in the Old Testament and Quran, etc.[1]

It is not "racist" to criticize any religion.

When all else fails, the trump card some religions prefer to use is to call you a racist if you mention that their identity group is violent, discriminatory or merely question its tenets or validity.

Islam is not a race. No religion is a race. Indeed, as Wikipedia kindly

---

[1] Links to horrible quotes in the Quran: http://www.thereligionofpeace.com/quran/023-violence.htm. Links to horrible quotes from the Bible: http://www.evilbible.com/Evil Bible Quotes.htm. For mroe on "The Old Testament is still valid": http://www.evilbible.com/do_not_ignore_ot.htm.

points out, "There is a wide consensus that the racial categories that are common in everyday usage are socially constructed, and that racial groups cannot be biologically defined." In other words, the very concept of "race" is questionable. Meanwhile, we agree that some people have dark skin, some people have brown or light skin, and facial features may vary; these are things that you are born into and a black or white person can't suddenly leave his "race," if we want to use that term. On the other hand, countless individuals have left their religions, or, indeed, joined different religions.

"You just deny God because you want to sin without feeling guilty!"

I am actually really confused by this argument, since it implies that you do believe in God, and furthermore, in their particular version of God. It really seems as if this is denial on the theist's side instead, or that they may have not thought this through (as opposed to their other arguments, which they have thought through...).

Dialog 1

> Duke: You just deny God because you want to sin!

> Romus: This would imply that I actually believe in a god, and furthermore you probably mean your particular version of God. How would denying this god help me, though, if it did exist? After all, I'd still go to hell. Perhaps it is YOU who are denying the mighty Poobah because you're afraid of his true glory?

Dialog 2

> Rachel: You just deny God because you feel you're unworthy of Him!

> Sam: Which particular god am I denying, though? People have believed in thousands of deities over time.

> Rachel: *The* God!

> Sam: Vishnu?

> Rachel: You know which one I'm talking about!

> Sam: Yes, I do, but the way you're talking implies that your belief is somehow superior to the beliefs of billions of other people.

> Rachel: Those other gods are false gods and abominations! Deuteronomy 32:17 ESV says, "They sacrificed to demons that were no gods, to gods they had never known, to new gods that had come recently, whom your fathers had never dreaded."

Here we see that Rachel went on to justify her superiority by quoting her Bible. Please see "Being bombarded with religious verses" earlier in the book for countermeasures to being quoted holy texts.

If all else fails....

> Rachel: I still think you just want to sin and in the depths of your heart you know God is real.

> Sam: This reminds me of a story: In Eastern Europe, a man in his twenties was sitting with his grandfather: an old man of 80 years who survived the Second World War and was an ardent communist. "What garbage, this capitalism!" he exclaimed. "It's turned the world rotten! Back in my day, people were fair and treated each other with respect!"

> "I'd never want to go back to communism," said the younger man. "There are so many more opportunities now, and while it is indeed riskier and you may end up a failure, that makes people try harder and makes succeeding so much more worthwhile."

> "Bah! You're just saying that, either because you think you're smarter or better than everyone else and you want a bigger share, or because you don't want to live up to the socialist values of fairness, honesty and comradery!" replied the old man.

"Things would be terrible if there was no God!"

Loaded statement. This implies that there already is some sort of god without which things could be worse in comparison to the current state of affairs, in which said god exists. One may instinctively attempt to go down the path of "but things will be fine without God!" and give reasons — this is already incorrect, since by doing so you are tacitly agreeing with the notion that there is a god.

> Carl: But if there were no God, the world would be such an awful place!

> Joe Stein: you're implying that there already is a god, and the disappearance of said God would cause terrible consequences. There are thousands, nay, millions of concepts of gods — which one are you talking about?

> Carl: The Biblical god!

> Joe: But what about Vishnu or Ganesh? Wouldn't things be terrible if they didn't exist?

> Carl: But you don't believe in those gods, and neither do I, so

how is that relevant?

Joe: There are billions of people with different beliefs, and somehow not believing in your particular version of God or even any god at all seems to suit many people just fine.

Carl: Yes, but what I mean is, if there wasn't this guiding force to keep everything in check, to guide humanity, regardless of what you call it, things would be bad — like a car without a driver.

Joe: Perhaps, instead of talking about the consequences of a god not existing, we should focus on whether or not one actually exists.

Carl: Okay, let's start there.

"I don't believe in any religion — I'm just 'spiritual'."

"Spiritual" is probably the most slippery word that there is. Whenever you get this, either as a reply to one of your criticisms of faith or religion, or right from the outset, it's vital to stop and ask the subject to clarify what they mean by "spiritual." Chances are, they themselves won't know or will give you a vague and unsatisfying answer. Point out that "spiritual" can mean almost anything to anyone, and is usually a placeholder for "I have some vague beliefs about a soul, an afterlife and perhaps some benevolent but extremely vague god." Often, people with such vague beliefs might mix in concepts from other religions, such as *karma* or *chi* — this is "Salad Bar Theism," where you create your religious views by taking only the bits that you like from different religions. I myself was a "Salad Bar Theist" before I realized that it didn't make much sense.

Only once you know what the other person is talking about, by clarifying what he means by certain iffy words, can a real dialogue be held.

Dialog 1

Maj: You know, I don't subscribe to any particular religion — I'm just "spiritual."

GoodMan: Interesting — what exactly do you mean by spiritual?

Dialog 2

Ted: I consider myself a "spiritual" person.

Mark: "Spiritual" seems to be a very vague term that can mean almost anything. Sometimes it boils down to a cover for "I'm not really sure what I believe in — possibly souls, an afterlife, and perhaps a god as well as other concepts, but I haven't given it much thought, actually, and I'm not too sure about them, so I'll use this poetic label that everyone accepts."

Dialog 3

Jill: I consider myself a spiritual person.

Twain: Can you please elaborate on what "being spiritual" means to you? It's a very vague term that can mean different things to different people.

"I would sin if there was no God!"

Claims that people wouldn't behave as "well" as they currently do if they were to stop believing fall under this category of argument:

"If there was no God, I'd still be drinking."

"I would steal, murder and rape if there was no God!"

If we were to take these statements at face value, we'd have to say the theists were criminal at heart, since the only thing that leads them to behave ethically is that "dictator in the sky." However, I take issue with the notion that they are actually bad people. I remember making the same argument myself, while I was still a believer — what seems to occur is that people have the expectation of this "worst case scenario" of themselves, combined with not understanding where their morals actually come from: not from "up there" but from inside their own minds and from society.

Indeed, what struck me the most after I become an atheist was how little my morals had actually changed. For instance, to this day I am still a vegetarian, even though I no longer believe in the concept of karma. So, do not automatically think of people who make this argument as "deplorable"; it's simply that they do not yet have a good understanding of the origins of their own morality, and they fear that it could suddenly disappear.

Jack: If it turned out that there was no God, I would probably do all sorts of terrible things like murder and rape — there would no longer be any meaning in life.

Ryan: I actually don't believe you. I know you think you could do those things, but I see that you're a good person, and if you stop believing, you will be surprised how little your morals will change — if at all.

Jack: Thank you... I guess — but what are you basing that on? I still think I'd do those things.

Ryan: Well, I have not heard of a single case of people deconverting and suddenly going on killing sprees — many people seem to have this preconception, but it's just based on a misunderstanding of human nature and thinking that your morals will suddenly "disappear" if you stop believing, which is patently not the case.

Jack: So your morals remained exactly the same?

Ryan: Mostly, except I no longer have the feelings of guilt and worthlessness that some religions bestow upon people. No murders or rapes, as far as I recall.

Jack: *chuckles*

The origins of human morality are discussed more deeply in the chapter "Atheism and Morality."

"How can we know anything at all?"

Once every defense is broken and faith shown to be a shoddy type of epistemology, a theist might bring on this "nuclear" option, attacking all knowledge. It has many phrasings, but the quintessence is this:

> *"This world is so complex- it could all be a dream or we could be in the matrix, could science be wrong? How can we be sure we are all not totally deluded?"*

Matt Dillahunty of *The Atheist Experience* appropriately named this "An attack on knowing." It is an attempt to discredit all epistemologies, declaring them worthless.

We of course can't be sure that we aren't "In the Matrix" or any other such scenario, since that would be intellectually dishonest, and all that we can do is assume, "for now," that we're not. It would only be worth spending energy to defeat such an argument if we have an actual reason, based upon observation and evidence, that something like that may be the case:

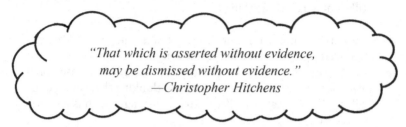

> *"That which is asserted without evidence,*
> *may be dismissed without evidence."*
> —Christopher Hitchens

Epistemologies are tools for finding out about the world, for building a better understanding of reality. There can be good tools and there can be fake tools. A good example of a fake tool is the "ADE 651" which was sold as a bomb detector. It is more or less a piece of plastic with a metal arrow sticking out that can swivel around — it purports to point towards bombs; however, in reality the metal arrow merely swings because the person holding it is not holding it perfectly still. In essence, it is a very expensive dowsing rod. It cost countless lives after being introduced to countries such as Iraq, where it allowed many suicide bombers to pass undetected through security checkpoints. The creator was since sentenced to ten years in prison in 2013.

Faith is just such a fake bomb detector: it purports to lead us to "the truth," however it ends up misleading us into the loss of human life, ignorance, heartbreak and false hope. The scientific method, on the other hand, is a good tool, since it demonstrably produces real results. This allows us to create new inventions such as airplanes, to understand the world better, to get rid of superstitions and false beliefs. It is thanks to the scientific method that we now have modern medicine to keep us healthy and prologue our lives, tall buildings to keep us safe from the elements, and nice glowing rectangles to keep us entertained. Next time, ask a theist why he needs to use a mobile phone if he has "faith."

How can we be sure we are not deluded or in the Matrix? We can't. I don't know that I'm not a brain in a mad-scientist's laboratory or that the world around me is not merely my dream. This is not a victory for a believer, anyway, since faith is a faulty way of knowing things (see "The Argument from Faith").

"You are too close-minded to see God"

Indeed, it is the theist who is usually being the "close-minded" one in this situation, since you as an atheist actually CAN imagine a universe where a god exists, and it would be much different to the universe we live in today: there would be no mosquitoes for one thing, there would be ONE, and only ONE holy text that everyone would agree upon — or even better, there would be no need for a text at all, since God would speak to everyone and everyone would actually get the same message, not "their interpretation" or "their opinion" — it would be analogous to Skype but inside your head.

Mindy: You are just too close-minded to See God.

Jake: Interesting — which one in particular?

Mindy: The God! There is only one!

Jake: Right, but can you describe him? Is it the god of the Bible?

Mindy: Yes!

Jake: See, here is where we run into a problem: there are thousands of Christian denominations in the US alone, many of which promise hell for those of other denominations, and the definition of God varies from person to person, and depends highly on their personality. I'm all for being "open-minded" — but not to such an extent that my brain falls out.

Mindy: I understand, but they're all actually praying to one God.

Jake: Well, the world has polytheists for one thing, also many branches of Buddhism are atheistic, not to mention all of the less common tribal religions where anything goes... My point is — say a Hindu approached you and asked you to worship Ganesh — would you be willing to do it?

Mindy: No, talking animals are an abomination, from the devil.

Jake: You say that, but you also implied that I was the close-minded one — the Hindu would probably say that it was indeed you who is close-minded, since you need to have faith to accept Ganesh.

"Do you think you have ever sinned in your life?"

James: Do you think you have ever sinned in your life?

Kevin: Uh, I don't know, maybe?

James: Luckily, God is all merciful, and if you pray, you will be forgiven.

Kevin: Wait, what? Which god?

This is a loaded question, and is a tactic for converting people to your particular religion. If you get asked this, you are being proselytized to. This is not a spontaneous or honest question, and it is likely that the person you are talking to learned this as part of his or her "training" for proselytizing.

By answering either "yes" or "no," you automatically admit that there is such a thing as "sin."

Sin: Deliberate disobedience to the known will of God.
- ThefreeDictioanry.com

As such, instead of answering the question, you should point out that this question is loaded, as it implies the existence of a god or pantheon against which it is possible to sin.

James: Do you think you have ever sinned in your life?

Kevin: Have I done things I'm not proud of and that I regret? Sure! However, "sin" would imply a deity that one can anger or transgress against, and I have not been convinced about the existence of any such deity.

If you did not use this maneuver and were to fall into that trap, you'd soon be hearing about how Jesus will still forgive you if you repent, join their church and pray hard enough.

"You atheists just hate God!"

This is not an argument per se, but an angry retort when the believer feels that his or her beliefs are threatened. It implies that a god that it is possible to hate exists, and that the interlocutor believes in that god.

Jill: Why do you atheists hate God so much?

Wayne: Wait — which one in particular are you referring to? The Christian god?

Jill: Yes, you know that.

Wayne: But why aren't you asking about Allah or Vishnu?

Jill: How is that relevant?

Wayne: Well, I don't believe in those either, so clearly I must "hate" them, as you say. Furthermore, it seems you hate them, too, under your logic.

Jill: They are manifestations of Satan, so, actually, yeah, I sort of do.

Wayne: This is interesting — I really want to see where you're coming from. So what if the Christian god is actually a satanic deception and Hinduism is the correct faith? You'd go to hell?

Jill: He's not.

Wayne: But how do you know?

Jill: I know because I have faith in the Bible.

There! She gave Wayne a hook! He can now explore why faith is not necessarily the greatest thing ever using the previously provided examples, and then "gracefully exit."

"Well, that's what other people of my faith believe in, not me."

We are each free to believe what we want to believe, but if someone chooses to call himself a Christian and yet not believe in the divinity of Christ, or that the Bible has been at least inspired by God, then we have a problem. You might be accused of being overly pedantic or intolerant — who are you to say who is or isn't a true Christian? But if a person who purports to belong to a particular faith actively disagrees with some of the core beliefs of that faith, it is not you who is at fault.

The appeal to shame

Oh my God! Can you believe he said that?? No really everyone look, he just said _____ !!! Did you really just say that?

When your interlocutor has not much to present in the form of a counter-argument, he may try to shame you into changing your position or into having you start making excuses for your views. The way to disarm this argument is to call the person out on it and not to back down. Let's look at two examples:

Dialog 1

Lilly: Did you really just say such a horrible thing? How can you say you don't believe that God is real and that Jesus died for your sins? What if someone else hears you?

Sam: I'm sorry, I didn't mean to offend you, but that is my real worldview.

Lilly: How can you actually believe that God doesn't exist? He made you and he made this planet — how can you be so ungrateful?

Sam: It's not that I'm ungrateful, I just don't believe.

Lilly: You just need to open your mind, and pray for goodness sake!

Dialog 2

Lilly: Did you really just say such a horrible thing? How can you say you don't think there is such a thing as God? What if someone else hears you?

Ann: My worldview seems to make you uncomfortable — which is unfortunate, but what you're trying to do — shaming me — won't work. If you have something of value to say, then we can talk about that.

Lilly: Of course it makes me uncomfortable! You can't just say such things, it is inappropriate.

Ann: You are so close-minded that you seem to experience allergic reactions to views which are contrary to your own; I don't wish to speak any further with you.

In the first dialogue, Sam tried to be polite and to "appease" Lilly. However, that only put her on the offensive, and the focus went toward discussing Sam and his "disrespectfulness." In the second dialogue, Ann, instead of apologizing, without resorting to emotional language, gave an overview of what was going on — that Lilly was getting uncomfortable and emotional, and she had none of it. She shifted the focus onto Lilly's close-mindedness, and terminated the conversation.

By becoming apologetic, you validate the framing that the theist has set up: that you said something wrong and that now an apology is expected from you. It doesn't help that you were trying to say it as non-combatively as possible — some theists that are not used to having their beliefs challenged will find any such discussion offensive in and of itself. In order to avoid having your ego trampled in such cases, it is important not to budge. Shift the focus of the discussion onto the believer and away from yourself. Doing so is not "dishonest" — it is a standard debate tactic. While it is best to avoid "debates" and instead follow the "therapist–patient" behavioral model that was previously described, this is an emergency technique you may need. Remember — this is not a scientific discussion where you both are honestly attempting to discern the mysteries of the cosmos. If you are getting an appeal to emotion of any kind, rather than a logical or semi-logical discussion, you don't have to sit there and take it.

It is wise not to interact with such people for very long, as stupidity is contagious. If you see that there is no reasoning with a person, it is best to simply leave.

Dealing with hypocritical (faux) skepticism

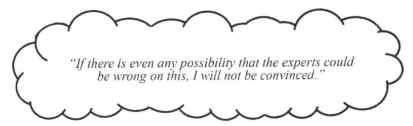

"If there is even any possibility that the experts could be wrong on this, I will not be convinced."

There is, oftentimes, this double standard of skepticism and the requirement of evidence when it comes to your claims and that of the theist. For instance, when you present an argument against creationism, or some instance of a supernatural or weird event in their holy book, or even against the use of faith, and the amount of "skeptical" pushback you might get towards your own claims will be an inordinate amount of times larger than any skepticism that the theist would possibly apply to himself — when this occurs, instead of appeasing the believer and continuing the discussion, point out the faux-skepticism.

Example Dialogue:

Jina: So do you really think there are no souls?

Mike: It would be great if there were an afterlife; however, all reputable medical knowledge points to the fact that when your brain is dead, so are you.

Jina: But don't you think medical knowledge is limited? Surely medicine doesn't know everything? (an attempt to begin an offensive push and push the skeptic into justifying himself) I cannot accept that the soul doesn't exist, unless there is not an ounce of doubt that it for sure doesn't exist. I am too skeptical of modern scientism — it can't know everything.

Mike: Yes, there is an immense amount of things we do not know yet — are you implying that you have a better way of knowing things? Why then don't you believe in Zeus, since we have not yet exhausted all hope of his existence? He might be on Mount Olympus somewhere. (Here he "calls her out on it." This discussion should then be directed to discussing why faith is an inadequate way of knowing things and "the graceful exit")

No True Scotsman

The No true Scotsman fallacy can be seen as the mirror opposite of "Well, that's what other people of my faith believe in, not me." It is an attempt to exclude all of the people that that the believer doesn't agree with from his religion, since those, according to the believer, are most certainly not "true" adherents of the faith. While we will look at religious examples, the actual fallacy can be found in much broader areas, including politics.

Mike: No Scotsman would ever refuse to eat meat!

Alex: Right, but my friend Billy is a Scotsman and he's a vegetarian.

Mike: Yes, but I mean no "true" Scotsman would ever refuse to eat meat.

Religious examples are aplenty, and believers within one religion can be quite certain that their co-religionists are severely misguided. This comes to light when an individual or group is manipulated into committing essentially political acts on the basis of their cherished religious beliefs. When it comes to terrorist acts, including the bombing of abortion clinics, most moderate religionists condemn the acts and consider the person involved to have a deeply flawed understanding of their religion. One word used to refer to such people is "miscreants." That is an interesting word, whose roots actually means wrong-believer. As Thefreedictionary.com says,

Miscreant

1. One who behaves badly, often by breaking rules of conduct or the law.
2. [Archaic] One who does not believe in a certain religion; an infidel or heretic.

Exercise Time! (Talking to Believers)

Think up a brief response:
  1. You are taking that passage out of context.

2. How dare you! You have no right to criticize the Bible!
3. You should read my holy book in full — otherwise you have no right to criticize my religion.
4. You are such a racist! You shouldn't criticize Islam.
5. You are saying that you don't believe in God, but I don't believe you — I just think you don't want to live according to his rules.
6. Don't you know that in Wiseman's 3:15 it says "And ye, skeptics, repent! For surely thou art misguided and feeble-minded!"

AVOIDING RELIGIOUS ARGUMENTS

In the previous chapter you learnt all about how to question your opponent's arguments and convince him that he "needs to do more research." However, debate is not always a valid option. There are many people you do not wish to argue with, for a variety of reasons, including other people's kids, the elderly, and the dying.

In these cases, we must also have a valid way to NOT debate, yet at the same time preserving our dignity and avoid feeling like a liar or hypocrite later on. Is this a tall order? Yes, it is, but it is doable.

First, let us list the various ways one might present himself during a religious discussion, from the most aggressive to the most passive:

1. Use of outright ridicule/profanities/racism.
2. Impassioned speech and logical argumentation.
3. Calm-speak and logical argumentation.
4. A "debate" where neither party dominates all of the time.
5. Being dominated/put down through religious argumentation.
6. Being outright ridiculed and insulted for your lack of beliefs.

While I recommend staying somewhere in the 2–4 range for most cases, those will not serve our purpose for this scenario. To avoid religious discussion altogether, I present to you the "avoidance tactic." For every religious statement that a person makes, you can:

1. Not respond.
2. Respond to the non-religious part of the statement.
3. Change the subject to something else.

These approaches should be used naturally and not with a sarcastic tone or as a clear sign of your disapproval.

The first and third are self-explanatory, but here are some examples of responding to non-religious parts of an argument:

Jake: I feel so worried about my job interview — I pray about it all the time!

Responding to the person:

Mike: You must really want that job. I'm sure the human

resources department will see that you're a great candidate.

Responding to the religion:

> Mike: Then instead of praying, why don't you actually do something useful — for instance exercise. You will worry a lot less.

> Melissa: I prayed and prayed, and through the power of Christ my daughter is now well again.

Responding to the person:

> Mike: You must really love her; I can see that you're a great mother.

Responding to the religion:

> Mike: It is through the power of the hard-working doctors and our medical system that she was cured, and you should thank them, instead of diverting all of the glory to your imaginary friend.

Of course, life can be unpredictable and you may be asked up-front about your beliefs: lie if you must, if your well-being depends on it, and don't feel burdened by it. The person who puts you in such a position shares the responsibility. Remember: it is much easier to avoid starting a discussion on religion than it is to end one amiably.

RELIGIONS 101

So far I have provided you with the "basis" of the atheistic worldview.[1] You hopefully now know where atheists get their morals from, why life is still meaningful, and how to counter general religious claims. The next part of the book will focus on giving you the "meat" of some of the most common religions that you might come in contact with.

Some of the books I found most useful include *The Heathen's Guide to World Religions* by William Hopper and *Lost Christianities: The Battles for Scripture and the Faiths We Never Knew* by Bart D. Ehrman. Here, I aim to give you the important bits that you, or indeed even the most devout believers, might not know about their own faiths, a kid of history that is accurate yet unfiltered and without any sort of respect for religions.

---

[1] Yes, I know that atheism is merely the lack of a belief in God(s). Here, by "atheistic worldview" I mean the common knowledge that the atheists of today will find useful.

The Evolution and History of the Judeo-Christian God

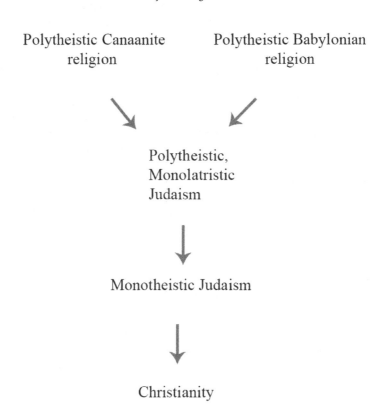

Polytheistic Canaanite
religion

Polytheistic Babylonian
religion

Polytheistic,
Monolatristic
Judaism

Monotheistic Judaism

Christianity

It may surprise you to find out that the god that the Christians, Jews and Muslims (and even the Mormons!!) worship has his roots in polytheism. That is, he was not always the single God that we have today, but was "*a god*," like Zeus. Indeed, way before the culture of Israel became a thing, there were these folks called Canaanites, that if you ever read the Bible you know the Jews were not too fond of, and therefore they slaughtered them. These Canaanites are important, because they pre-date the Jews, and they by the sheerest of coincidence also happen to have had a deity called "Yahweh" (to those that never bothered with the Bible, it is one of the names ascribed to the Jewish/Christian god). In the Canaanite tradition however, Yahweh was the War god — analogous to the Roman god Mars (this could explain why the Old Testament is so bloody and full of slaughter).

Indeed, the creation myth found in the Old Testament seems derived from the much (more than a thousand years) earlier Canaanite story where in the universe was also created "in order," and the same general ideas are seen, such as the firmament (the ancients thought that the sky was a physical dome-type-thing that they called "the firmament"). However, apart from having mere old Yahweh, the Canaanites also had a grocery list of other gods like all good self-respecting polytheists do. Indeed, some of them even made it into the Bibles we currently have — in particular, there is the "Baal" character, who is heavily denounced as an abomination in the Old Testament, but who for the Canaanites existed as a god of fertility, and another Ba'al figure was the god for storms.

The Baals, unlike almost every other god on that list, have surnames so as to avoid confusion. Also Yahweh had a wife! Imagine that! She was called Asherah. However, she was not only his wife — you see, in Sumerian communities she was considered the wife of Anu, who is the head god in *The Epic of Gilgamesh*. Now, before you get lost in all of these names: there used to be plenty of gods, not just Yahweh, that different cultures "borrowed," slightly modified and included in their pantheons. Indeed, deities with the same names could exist in several cultures and have somewhat different stories — it was the ultimate free-for-all of deity copying. Something like that would surely not be allowed today, with the copyright laws and all.

Now, all of that begins to change a bit later, when the Hebrews lost a few battles and got driven out, however instead of thinking that this was the end of their culture and god (in those days, gods were tied to locales/cities, so the loss of a city meant the death of a god), the Hebrews decided to flip the script — that this was actually their god Yahweh demonstrating his power and showing them he was annoyed with them for not worshiping him enough. In those days people were generally illiterate and there was no notion of religious freedom or war crimes. Anyhow, over the years the Hebrews became *monolatristic* — which means that they now worshipped just one god, even though they thought that other gods still exist — this is like allying yourself with a political party: you don't deny the existence of other political parties, but you oppose them. Indeed, the Ten Commandments still have this trace of monolatrism:

> "Though shalt have no other gods before me"

This implies that there are other gods, which one at his peril could *have* before Yahweh. It was only much later that Prophet Muhammad (PBUH) (PBUH is traditionally tagged after his name; it means "Peace be upon him") introduced the following notion:

> "There is no God but Allah and Muhammad (PBUH) is the Messenger of Allah."

Back to our discussion of the Hebrews — after a while this monolatrism became more and more extreme, eventually some king decided to erase the evidence of the other gods entirely and make it appear that it is only Yahweh that exists and should be worshipped. Indeed, there are still some remnants of those gods in the Bible: do you know all of those different fancy names for God that are present in the Bible? Many of those used to be distinct gods. Indeed, "Elohim," a term which is present in the Bible and is used as another name for God, was previously used to refer to an assembly of various gods.[1] Also, and I don't know if this was changed from the original, but I find that it annoys Christians when I ask "When God said that 'Let there be Light!' — who was he talking to?"

I didn't choose the title of this section as a metaphor — religions do evolve, and this is what makes them successful, and what allows them to have so much impact of humanity: it is the "survival of the fittest" in the battlefield of ideas.

Imagine two hypothetical ancient tribes: one tribe has a religious doctrine of "be peaceful and do not attack no matter what," the other has the doctrine of "though shalt spread the word of the lord and conquer the infidels." If these two tribes were to be placed next to each other, can we venture a guess into the religion in that area in a few hundred years? I say yes. When we talk about the evolution of ideas, it is the "fittest" idea that survives, and the natural ones get selected out. The ones that survive are the ones that are most adept at spreading, either through literal battle, through "preaching the word" or through creating such conditions where the adherents of this religion create new adherents through breeding faster than competing ones.

Religions can't offer a good source of morality, due to the fact that once written down "the word" cannot be changed, they can only be interpreted or ignored away. The texts, or indeed the "interpretations" of texts also change — what was once useful or pertinent, like stoning your child for misbehaving, keeping slaves, the second-class status of women, has been interpreted away as not relevant or as "no longer applicable," as being poetry, as something that is "not meant to be taken literally," or downright ignored. Depending on the religion in question, parts may even be erased, or new books added. If we were to look at this from a "Well, what did God really say?" perspective then this all looks rather horrid — as a corruption of the faith, where only the most ardent fundamentalists have any chance of salvation. However, this is actually perfectly natural and expected if we look at it not from a truth/falsehood perspective, but from the perspective of ideas that constantly need to reinvent themselves to survive in new environments: the old ideas and ways of doing things go out of fashion and are deemed "immoral," and the new more enlightened worldview of the adherents gets interpreted into the faith.

---

[1] http://en.wikipedia.org/wiki/Elohim

Additional Resources:
- *The Heathen's Guide to World Religions* By William Hopper
- *Lost Christianities: The Battles for Scripture and the Faiths We Never Knew* by Bart D. Ehrman
  - *Who Wrote the Bible?* by Richard Elliott Friedman

EVALUATING CHRISTIAN VALUES

The Ten Commandments

Christians claim that their morality comes from the Bible, and more specifically, the Ten Commandments (there is no actual list of the Ten Commandments in the Bible, and indeed there is only a vague mention that there are ten such commandments in Exodus and in Deuteronomy. The Old Testament contains around 613 commandments, so which of those are the "true 10" is anyone's guess. The Abrahamic faiths take their commandments from Exodus 20:1–17[1] and Deuteronomy 5:4–21.[2] The problem is that there is no "And here are the Ten Commandments" part — instead all of these commandments are listed haphazardly, and there are many more than ten.

For instance, why is this not a commandment?

> Exodus 20:26 KJV
>
> *Neither shalt thou go up by steps unto Mine altar, that thy nakedness be not uncovered thereon*

This seems to be a perfectly reasonable "command" — do not go naked unto God's altar. I'm sure I will be hearing from countless apologists telling me how wrong I am and how it is "obvious" that the current selection of the 10 Commandments is valid.

Anyhow, let's stop worrying about how inconsistent their origin is and examine them point by point:

1. I am the Lord thy God.

Okay? Can you prove it? If any God(s) exist out there then can I please have a sandwich appear in front of me as I'm typing this? Mmm, no sandwich... too bad...

2. Thou shalt have no other gods before me.

---

[1] Exodus 20:1–17   http://www.mechon-mamre.org/p/pt/pt0220.htm
[2] Deuteronomy 5:4–21,   http://www.mechon-mamre.org/p/pt/pt0505.htm

This actually implies that other gods do exist, which one could presumably choose to respect more than Yahweh/Jehovah. This is a relic from the polytheistic origins of the Hebrew faith.[1] Why would an omnipotent being feel threatened if a mere mortal, an ant in comparison, should mistakenly worship a delusion? We are not threatened by the worldviews of ants, which seem infinitely simple and unimportant when compared to our own worldviews.

3. Thou shalt not make unto thee any graven image.

Depending on the interpretation, this means either not worshiping idols or indeed not having any type of statue/wood carving. Either way, Christians break this constantly by having religious icons that are indeed graven, as well as statues of Jesus, Mary, and the like. While Christians will adamantly reply that these are not idols but mere representations, the distinction seems very iffy to me, especially considering that the above text merely says "graven images." And many Christians feel compelled to make the sign of the cross when they come across such images, or even when they walk past a church. Muslims have everything better sorted, with strict prohibitions on religious imagery.

4. Thou shalt not take the name of the Lord thy God in vain.

It seems that the Hebrew/Christian/Islamic god also has pride issues — I personally wouldn't feel threatened or angered if, say, a small child were to use my name in vain or even call me a poo-poo head. However, the supposedly omnipotent deity views this as a great threat — this only makes sense when viewing God as a mere ephemeral idea that can be challenged by other ideas — an omnipotent deity wouldn't care.

5. Remember the Sabbath day, to keep it holy.

The problem with "the Sabbath day" is that there is ample disagreement among the various Abrahamic faiths about what day of the week it actually is, and about the exact meaning of "keeping it holy."[2] However, the actual word "Sabbath" comes from the Greek word "Sabato," which means "Saturday."

6. Honor thy father and thy mother.

This has a semblance of being reasonable; however the problem lies with its absoluteness: for example what if your father was a drug-user/alcoholic that raped you, and your mother consumed heroin which caused you developmental difficulties, after which she gave you up for adoption? Should you still honor them? Honor needs to be earned.

7. Thou shalt not kill.

This is also very subjective: for instance, the ancient Hebrews did not consider killing during war "murder." Also, what about killing for self-defense or to save lives? This commandment also doesn't say "Thou shalt not kill humans," so should we all become vegetarians and spare even the lives of flies and mosquitoes, the way Jains do?

---

[1] Yahweh as part of a pantheon: http://en.wikipedia.org/wiki/Canaanite_religion
[2] http://en.wikipedia.org/wiki/Sabbath

8. Thou shalt not commit adultery.

I am all for a faithful marriage. This makes quite a lot of sense; however, what does not make much sense is the punishment — death:

> "Behold, you are a dead man because of the woman whom you have taken, for she is a man's wife."
>
> — Genesis 20:3 (ESV)

9. Thou shalt not steal.

This is a good idea on the face of it, but again I have an issue with its absoluteness — what if someone was about to die of hunger and you had no money but could steal a loaf of bread. Or how about this: a giant corporation made a virus that would kill everyone except for a select few with the antidote — would it be wrong to steal that antidote from that corporation to save mankind? Those are extreme examples, but this is how one tests these things out — an omnipotent deity has supposedly written this, so the commandment could have been "Thou shalt not steal, except for situations where ___."

10.   Thou shalt not bear false witness against thy neighbor.

(This one seems pretty reasonable.)

11.   Thou shalt not covet your neighbors' wife/female servant/male servant/field/donkey.

Depending on the passage, this refers to coveting (desiring) your neighbor's wife, female servant, male servant, field. This commandment is of the "thought-police" kind — there is nothing wrong with desire and fantasy, as long as it's within the confines of your imagination. Had this commandment been something to the effect of "Though shalt not plot to steal your neighbor's ___," I would have found it much more reasonable.

How are there 11 commandments? Well, different Christian traditions use them in different sequences, and some traditions use different ones — I included all of them for completeness.[1]

What the Bible/Old Testament says about various issues

Note: these laws are from the Old Testament, but don't let that fool you — if any of the Old Testament laws were abolished by Jesus, it would be the sacrificial laws. The 10 Commandments are also from the Old Testament.

---

[1] http://en.wikipedia.org/wiki/Ten_Commandments

"For truly, I say to you, till heaven and earth pass away, not an iota, not a dot, will pass the law until all is accomplished. Whoever then relaxes one of the least of these commandments and teaches men so, shall be called least in the kingdom of heaven; but he who does them and teaches them shall be called great in the kingdom of heaven." (Matthew 5:18-19 RSV)

"It is easier for Heaven and Earth to pass away than for the smallest part of the letter of the law to become invalid." (Luke 16:17 NAB)

The Crime: Being disobedient to your parents

The Punishment: You get stoned to death.

Deuteronomy 21:18-21
King James Version (KJV)
18 If a man have a stubborn and rebellious son, which will not obey the voice of his father, or the voice of his mother, and that, when they have chastened him, will not hearken unto them:

19 Then shall his father and his mother lay hold on him, and bring him out unto the elders of his city, and unto the gate of his place;
20 And they shall say unto the elders of his city, This our son is stubborn and rebellious, he will not obey our voice; he is a glutton, and a drunkard.
21 And all the men of his city shall stone him with stones, that he die: so shalt thou put evil away from among you; and all Israel shall hear, and fear.

The Crime: Being gay

The punishment: Death!

"If a man lies with a male as with a women, both of them shall be put to death for their abominable deed; they have forfeited their lives." (Leviticus 20:13 NAB)

In various passages death penalties are prescribed for people who don't want to listen to what the priests tell them to do, as well as for witches, gays (and lesbians), fornicators (pre-marital sex), and false prophets — all of these laws are not worthy of today's society.[1]

---

[1] For all of the specific passages visit http://www.evilbible.com/Murder.htm

The Crime: Converting to a different religion or trying to convert others to a different religion

The result: You get stoned! (This is becoming a pattern.)

Deuteronomy 13:6-10
King James Version (KJV)
6 If thy brother, the son of thy mother, or thy son, or thy daughter, or the wife of thy bosom, or thy friend, which is as thine own soul, entice thee secretly, saying, Let us go and serve other gods, which thou hast not known, thou, nor thy fathers;

7 Namely, of the gods of the people which are round about you, nigh unto thee, or far off from thee, from the one end of the earth even unto the other end of the earth;

8 Thou shalt not consent unto him, nor hearken unto him; neither shall thine eye pity him, neither shalt thou spare, neither shalt thou conceal him:
9 But thou shalt surely kill him; thine hand shall be first upon him to put him to death, and afterwards the hand of all the people.

10 And thou shalt stone him with stones, that he die; because he hath sought to thrust thee away from the Lord thy God, which brought thee out of the land of Egypt, from the house of bondage.

The Bible's position on slavery

The Bible allows slavery, pure and simple. There are slightly differing conditions for Jews who are enslaved (who must be freed after seven years, unless they so happen to fall in love with another slave of their master, and if they choose to marry her they are then forever enslaved), however don't let anyone fool you into that they were merely "indentured servants" and that it "has to be viewed in context." Owners of their slaves were allowed to have sex with them and beat them so long as they didn't die.

Having multiple wives

Well, naturally that's allowed — there are many instances of polygamy in the Bible and nowhere is it condemned.

However, you may purchase male or female slaves from among the foreigners who live among you. You may also purchase the children of such resident foreigners, including those who have been born in your land. You may treat them as your property, passing them on to your children as a permanent inheritance. You may treat your slaves like this, but the people of Israel, your relatives, must never be treated this way. (Leviticus 25:44-46 NLT)

When a man strikes his male or female slave with a rod so hard that the slave dies under his hand, he shall be punished. If, however, the slave survives for a day or two, he is not to be punished, since the slave is his own property. (Exodus 21:20-21 NAB)

Slaves, obey your earthly masters with deep respect and fear. Serve them sincerely as you would serve Christ. (Ephesians 6:5 NLT)

Nowhere does it say something like "Though shalt not own slaves." Do not let Christian apologists fool you by saying that it was "a different time" — there is no "proper time" for slavery.

Wearing cloth from mixed fabric, eating shellfish is strictly off-limits!

Leviticus 19:19
King James Version (KJV)
19 Ye shall keep my statutes. Thou shalt not let thy cattle gender with a diverse kind: thou shalt not sow thy field with mingled seed: neither shall a garment mingled of linen and woollen come upon thee.

Leviticus 11:10
And all that have not fins and scales in the seas, and in the rivers, of all that move in the waters, and of any living thing which is in the waters, they shall be an abomination unto you

There are of course "good" passages in the Bible/Torah, however today's Christians use their own judgment as to which ones apply in today's world and which ones are "metaphorical/no longer apply." That comes close to choosing secular morals which are based on logic and reason.

Additional Resources:
- www.EvilBible.com
- www.SkepticsAnnotatedBible.com
- Matt Dillahunty: The Superiority of Secular Morality (YouTube Video)

THE CHANGING PROHIBITIONS OF CHRISTIANITY

With the current focus on gays, it's easy to overlook other things that today are deemed acceptable in Christianity that were once horrendous and despicable sins.

Usury

Religions seem to hate usury (the lending of money at interest, meaning you get back a bit more than you lent, in return for the risk of possibly not getting anything at all back since the person you gave it to might run away). Usury is condemned, banned or frowned upon in the Vedic Texts, Buddhism, Judaism, Islam and Christianity. While the Islamic ban on usury still holds, most Christians and Jews now happily ignore it.

> *Exodus 22:25*
>
> *If you lend money to any of my people with you who is poor, you shall not be like a moneylender to him, and you shall not exact interest from him.*

> *Deuteronomy 23:19*
>
> *Thou shalt not lend upon usury to thy brother;
> usury of money, usury of victuals, usury of any
> thing that is lent upon usury.*

Eating pork

Jews and Muslims don't eat pork, because the Old Testament writings call it an "abomination." (Christians get a pass, on this, because that proscription is over-ruled in the New Testament.)

> Isaiah 66:15-17 ESV
>
> *"For behold, the Lord will come in fire, and his chariots like the whirlwind, to render his anger in fury, and his rebuke with flames of fire. For by fire will the Lord enter into judgment, and by his sword, with all flesh; and those slain by the Lord shall be many. "Those who sanctify and purify themselves to go into the gardens, following one in the midst, eating pig's flesh and the abomination and mice, shall come to an end together, declares the Lord.*

The *New Testament* has many quotes, however, that go against the old teachings:

> Romans 14:14 ESV
>
> *I know and am persuaded in the Lord Jesus that nothing is unclean in itself, but it is unclean for anyone who thinks it unclean.*

Still, if one were to take the Bible seriously, one would be wary of these contradictory passages and abstain from doing anything that could potentially land you in an eternity of torment.

Tattoos

Know of anyone with a tattoo of Jesus or of Bible quotes? Those are abominations as well:

> Leviticus 19:28 KJV
> *Ye shall not make any cuttings in your flesh for the dead, nor print any marks upon you: I am the LORD.*

Divorce

> Luke 16:18 ESV
> *"Everyone who divorces his wife and marries another commits adultery, and he who marries a woman divorced from her husband commits adultery.*

> Romans 7:2 ESV
> *For a married woman is bound by law to her husband while he lives, but if her husband dies she is released from the law of marriage.*

> Mark 10:12 ESV
> *And if she divorces her husband and marries another, she commits adultery."*

To paraphrase, divorce equals adultery, and adultery equals getting executed. Divorces in Europe finally began to gain legal acceptance during the end of 1700s; however there was still a long way to go, with divorce being viewed as socially unacceptable and legally permissible only in very specific cases. These days, you would not be to hard-pressed to find people that profess the Christian faith that have had multiple divorces — a crime that would have earned them several death sentences in the past.

Eating seafood that is not fish

This verse comes from Leviticus — the same book where homosexuality is so strongly condemned. The selective application of Old Testament morality is rife in today's society, with this verse being totally ignored since seafood is so tasty.

> Leviticus 11:10
> *And all that have not fins and scales in the seas, and in the rivers, of all that move in the waters, and of any living thing which is in the waters, they shall be an abomination unto you*

Wearing mixed fabrics

You are forbidden from wearing garments that are made of combinations of different materials.

> Deuteronomy 22:11
> *Thou shalt not wear a garment of divers sorts, as of woollen and linen together.*

Having a rounded haircut

To be fair, North Korea also has a list of approved haircuts: 18 styles for women and 10 for men.

> Leviticus 19:27
> *Ye shall not round the corners of your heads, neither shalt thou mar the corners of thy beard.*

Anything to do with mediums, ghosts and fortune-telling

> Leviticus 19:31
> *Regard not them that have familiar spirits, neither seek after wizards, to be defiled by them: I am the LORD your God.*

If you know of any devout Christians who enjoy pork, non-fish based seafood, wearing clothes made of a combination of fabrics and perhaps are even divorced — well, they are as much destined for hell as any gays are. Throw out all of your gold, pearls, mobile phones and wearable gadgets just to be safe as well.

Wearing gold or pearls

> 1 Timothy 2:9
> *In like manner also, that women adorn themselves in modest apparel, with shamefacedness and sobriety; not with broided hair, or gold, or pearls, or costly apparel*

This means no technology like iPhones or Google Glass either, since those are both "costly apparel" and also may contain gold for the microchips.

Women teachers or women with power/authority are an abomination

If you are a fortune-telling woman who has power over men, teaches, or wears gold, pearls and expensive clothes, then you are destined for hell!

1 Timothy 2:12
*But I suffer not a woman to teach, nor to usurp authority over the man,
but to be in silence.*

Many Christian denominations, as well as Jews and Muslims, do adhere to many of the above prohibitions, however the sheer amount of pointless prohibitions means there will always be things that are conveniently forgotten about.

The Puritans banned Christmas

In mid-17th century England, the Puritans deemed Christmas "wasteful" and considered it tied to the Catholic Church, and of overall not being somber — too much fun. They would patrol the streets, imposing fines and punishment on anyone deemed too "merry," confiscating any Christmasy food and making all of the shops stay open on Christmas to avoid people going home to celebrate. The person responsible for all of this was none other than Oliver Cromwell. After his death, he was buried with full honors; however, he was so despised that his dead body was later dug up and decapitated. After Charles the Second was restored to the throne, all of the merrymaking resumed. Next time someone mentions "The War on Christmas," be sure to enlighten them with this here tale.

The Firmament, Sky and Heavens

L'atmosphère: météorologie populaire (1888)

In the Bible and in the Quran, the sky is viewed as a solid dome, which prevents the waters from above from falling onto the earth in undue quantities (the notion that clouds actually contain water seems to have eluded them). The stars are holes in said wall, through which you can look into the heavens.

> *Then God said, "Let there be a firmament in the midst of the waters, and let it divide the waters from the waters." Thus God made the firmament, and divided the waters which were under the firmament from the waters which were above the firmament; and it was so. And God called the firmament Heaven. So the evening and the morning were the second day*

> Then God said, "Let there be a space between the waters, to separate the waters of the heavens from the waters of the earth."

The Ascension, by Dosso Dossi, 16th century.

167

There seems to have been no distinction between "the sky" and "the heavens" in the Bible — that is, the current view that most Christians have of heaven as "some other dimension" is a totally new invention. Before the invention of flight, the images of heaven as "people and angels atop of clouds" was not symbolical or metaphorical — people took that completely literally. It is only after we started flying atop of clouds that their sheer emptiness made us transition to the whole "heaven is not directly in the sky, but rather another world, or perhaps the people on the clouds are invisible since it is just their spirits" worldview.

CHRISTIAN COUNTER-APOLOGETICS

It is best not to delve too deeply into the specifics of any religion, and instead to work on the believer's faith as described in the "Counter-Apologetics" chapter. However, it is still worth being educated on specific religions. This book does not aim examine every part of the Bible or even any significant amount of it — for that you can read *The Skeptics Annotated Bible* by Steve Wells. However, we can address the claims that many Christians make. Make no mistake — different Christians can have vastly different views, from the hardcore biblical literalist who believes that the creation story, flood story, the story of the tower of Babel were all historical events and that the earth is six to ten thousand years old, to the "fluffy theist" who believes that there is "some force behind the universe that loves us" and that "Jesus was probably an enlightened man that existed some time ago." The "Counter-Apologetics" chapter dealt with more generalized arguments, whereas this chapter and the next one on Islam will deal with those arguments that are more localized to those religions.

Christianity isn't a religion — it's a relationship/philosophy

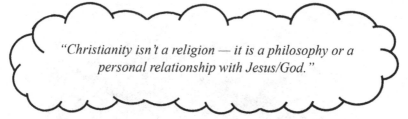

"Christianity isn't a religion — it is a philosophy or a personal relationship with Jesus/God."

This is often presented to deflect any general criticism you might have and attempt to present Christianity as something different and personal. As Matt Dillahunty of the *Atheist Experience* asked: "If Christianity isn't a religion, then shouldn't we tax the churches?" Suddenly, when things come down to taxes and money, it magically becomes a religion; this is not too dissimilar from the wave-particle duality property of light, which acts as either one or the other depending on whether there is an observer.

Also, let's pause for a minute and think of what "relationship" means. Relationships usually involve two or more people dealing with each other in some way, acting upon each other, communicating with each other.

Let's say I were to tell you that I'm great friends with Richard Dawkins. You would naturally inquire how often we talk and what sorts of things we discuss, where we meet, and whether you might meet him as well. However, if I said, "it's a more transcendent friendship than that: we do not communicate directly, instead I read his books and sing about him on the streets." You'd think I was crazy — but somehow this sort of one-sided relationship with Jesus gets a pass.

Dialog 1

> James: See, Christianity isn't a religion; instead I have a personal relationship with Jesus.

> Mark: Wow, how often do you two talk? What's he like?

> James: Now, you're just mocking me, you know what I mean.

> Mark: See, for words to mean things, we have to agree on definitions. If I were to tell you that I had a relationship with George Bush, and that it consists of me writing emails to him and watching him on television, you'd consider me crazy. A relationship consists of people actually talking to each other, or at least communicating in some fashion.

Dialog 2

> Timmy: See, I don't see Christianity as a religion. I consider it more of a link between myself and God.

> Cassandra: So if Christianity isn't a religion, will it be OK if we tax the churches then?

Furthermore, this argument is rendered nonsensical if we look at the etymology of the word "religion." It dates back from the Roman word "religio," which meant "obligation," "bond" and reverence. So if we take that sentence again, and replace the word "religion" with its actual meaning, it means "Christianity isn't a bond with God, it is a relationship" — which is self-defeating. Perhaps, though, the proponent of this argument means "organized religion" in the sense of going to a specific type of church and being part of a Christian community. He may not participate in an "organized" or corporate religion, but most people of faith do.

Finally, according to "thefreedictionary.com," the first in the list of meanings for religion is:

> *"Belief in and reverence for a supernatural power or powers regarded as creator and governor of the universe."*

This means that the person claiming he is not "religious" but has a "relationship" with God or Jesus wants to say that he doesn't believe God/Christ are divine, but he has a relationship with them; or that he has no relationship with a dictionary.

The Bible is the inspired word of God, and the historicity of the Bible is well known and reliable.

Estimates vary as to when the New Testament was written; apparently some parts may date to AD 50 and the rest has been dated several hundred years after that. It consists of different documents written and was edited by different writers. Even to use the term "New Testament" prior to AD 325 would be misleading, as it was a collection of texts, with various Christian sects preferring various combinations of such texts. It was only in AD 325 that Emperor Constantine called the "First Council of Nicaea," where a group of religious leaders, under the guidance of the Holy Spirit, of course, decided which books would make it into the Bible and which were inconvenient to them.

The texts that didn't make it into the final version are called the Apocrypha. Initially, I thought I'd take some time and read them all. However, I soon realized that the material that could have been included in the Bible but was deliberately omitted was so voluminous that it would probably take many months or even years to read everything.

There are no contradictions in the Bible.

Even with the careful editing, the Bible is full of contradictions. Here is just one:

> *God is tired and rests*
> *Ex 31:17*
> *God is never tired and never rests*
> *Is 40:28*

One needs but to Google "Biblical contradictions" to get a large list. Theists may do logical acrobatics to explain them away, (especially, "it's a metaphor," or "it happened both ways", or "we're just too feeble-minded to understand the book correctly, since we are mere mortals and the Bible couldn't possibly be wrong"). The reply that "The Bible was written by the fallible hand of man and merely inspired by God," is not an answer but an excuse. Ask again if there are in fact contradictions, and if so, how we can know which part was intended by God.

God is Omni-benevolent (All-Loving), Omniscient (All-knowing), Omnipotent (All-powerful), Omnipresent (everywhere at the same time)

Something can't be "all-powerful." The ancient Greeks already raised the question, in the famous deity-and-rock problem, "If a deity is all-powerful, can it create a rock so large and heavy that it itself can't lift it"? If God did choose to create such a rock, he would no longer be all-powerful since he wouldn't be able to lift it, on the other hand if he wasn't able to create it he wouldn't be all-powerful in the first place: it's a lose-lose situation. Also apart from that example there is a mention in the Bible itself, of how God was defeated by iron chariots:

> And *the LORD* was with Judah; and he drove
> out the inhabitants of the mountain;
> but *could not drive out the inhabitants of the valley,*
> *because they had chariots of iron*

Also another problem that arises is the problem of evil. If God is all-loving and can see everything, then there should be no illness and bad things such as war in the world, since he is all-powerful. He is either not all-loving, since he allows suffering, or he is merely impotent.

An objection often raised to this is the problem of free will, couched in terms that suggest that if God were to stop all suffering and injustice, there would be no free will. However, this argument falls apart as well: I am not able to fly or shoot laser beams out of my eyes — does this mean I don't have "free will"? Power and free will are different things. Indeed, a paralyzed man who can only blink still has free will: he can choose when to blink, and more to the point, he can choose what to think. Removing the ability to cause terrible pain would not negate our free will.

"Archeologists have found the ark!"

Yes, the problem is that they keep finding it. Indeed, many poor communities make an industry out of selling "wood from the ark" or leading people on expeditions to find it. However, the problem is that these "findings" keep occurring in different parts of the world, and so far we have no reason believe that a global flood took place and that there exists an ark that survived such a flood. Reputable scientists/historians are no more impressed by this than by "UFO wreckage from area 51" or "Hair from Bigfoot."

"I believe because of all the prophecies in the Bible/Torah that came true!"

Ask for examples. Often the prophecy is either vague to the point of being useless, written after the fact, or is a self-fulfilling prophecy (for example, if I have a dream that tomorrow I'll eat noodle soup and I go out and buy noodle soup and eat it. Miracle!)

The Bible is socially progressive (anti-slavery, pro women's rights)

False, there is not one verse in the Bible saying anything to the effect of "free your slaves to go to heaven" — in fact, the opposite is true:

> *Slaves, obey your earthly masters with respect and fear, and with sincerity of heart, just as you would obey Christ. Ephesians 6:5*

Indeed the Bible goes into much detail about slave laws, including gems such as that if a Jewish slave has been with you for seven years (after which he is free to leave) but you find him a slave girl to fall in love with, he may ask you to stay and be your slave forever; you must then drive an "awl" (a sharp tool) through his ear at the door post, and he is yours forever. (Foreign slaves are yours forever by default.)

Women's issues are particularly problematic. If a man rapes a girl, he would be forced to marry her since she is now "damaged property." Also, he will have to pay the father (since she is his property) 50 shekels of silver (that may be somewhere near $500 today; a lot of money in an economy that was more geared to agriculture and self-sufficiency than to cash exchanges).

> *"If a man happens to meet a virgin who is not pledged to be married and rapes her and they are discovered, he shall pay the girl's father fifty shekels of silver. He must marry the girl, for he has violated (anah) her. He can never divorce her as long as he lives." Deuteronomy 22:28-29 NIV*

Surprisingly, Christian apologists will try to argue these points away, with comments such as "It was more analogous to indentured servitude and not the cotton plantation slavery we know" and "In those days having the rapist marry his victim was the only choice since no one else would marry her and provide for her." However, the fact that it happened long ago doesn't excuse slavery — to me, there is no "context" in which slavery is acceptable, or in which treating rape like property damage would be considered moral. If the god of the Old Testament was omnipotent and loving, we'd have lines such as "Though shalt not own a slave!" and "Women have the same legal rights as men!"

Exercise Time! (Biblical Counter-Apologetics)

Think up a brief response:
1. Historians have shown that the Bible is reliable.
2. The Bible has no internal contradictions.
3. The Bible supports women's rights and is against slavery.
4. The prophecies in the Bible are being fulfilled.
5.

> Additional Resources:
> - *A Manual for Creating Atheists* by Peter Boghossian
> - The Atheist Experience (online show)
> - The Magic Sandwich Show (online show)
> - "The Thinking Atheist" YouTube show

DEALING WITH CREATIONISM

When I first heard that around half of the population of the United States believes that the earth is 4,000–6,000 years old, my heart sank — it was like finding out that half of them believe in the Flat Earth model. Creationism usually goes hand in hand with the denial of evolution. Whenever these two are brought up, the most common response is to argue — that is, to attempt to "teach" your interlocutor about science. This usually ends up in a failure. It's not that the theist "did not know" about these scientific views beforehand; rather he knows about them and has had many misconceptions intentionally placed in his mind by his cultural milieu. In other words, he has been indoctrinated into believing that the science behind them is inherently flawed, or indeed, that "The evidence for evolution placed there by the devil to confuse everyone."

If you value your time, assert that there are many religious believers who do accept evolution, so the theist's "battle" is with them.

Dialog 1

Bradley: You need just as much faith to believe in evolution as I have in the Biblical creation.

Jill: False: I need no faith whatsoever. The current scientific consensus is that evolution is the best explanation so far — if tomorrow some discovery occurred that undermined the theory of evolution, that scientist would probably win a Nobel Prize. That, however, is unlikely, due to the staggering amount of evidence for evolution.

Bradley: So you believe whatever the scientists say — that's just the same as faith.

Jill: False again. Do you know how the scientific method works? If someone has a "neat idea" it is not yet science, and for something to be widely accepted fellow scientists first have to try to discredit it as much as possible, and only if it withstands their brutal scrutiny, *and* if other scientists are able to reproduce those results, it becomes accepted as the "best current understanding of something" — that is the exact opposite of faith.

Dialog 2

Jones: So you believe in evolution?

Mackay: I don't "believe" in it — the current scientific consensus is that is the best explanation so far. However, there are countless Christians that believe in evolution as well — so how is evolution relevant?

Jones: Well, there are many flaws in the theory of evolution...

Mackay: Wait, wait — let's say, for this discussion, that there was no such theory or that it was proven false. So what? That still doesn't provide evidence for the Christian god.

Jones: Right, but the Bible describes creation, so it is relevant.

Mackay: I think this particular discussion is best to be had between you and a fellow Christian who thinks evolution is the best explanation.

In this last discussion the interlocutor "expects" to be told the contrary viewpoint and simply "waits for you to finish talking" before moving on. But instead of "educating" the theist, which is an uphill battle to say the least, you provide something else entirely: you show that creationism and Christianity are not necessarily inseparable, and you shift the burden of the discussion from yourself onto a Christian, with whom the theist might be more comfortable talking about said matter. The route of least resistance and effort is key. You might run into the "well he's not a true Christian" fallacy though, which was discussed in the "Talking to Believers" chapter.[1]

---

[1] The fallacy itself is called "No True Scotsman," and is under that name in the Talking to Believers chapter.

The evolution of the eye

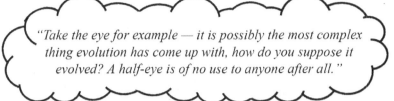

"Take the eye for example — it is possibly the most complex thing evolution has come up with, how do you suppose it evolved? A half-eye is of no use to anyone after all."

"What good is half an eye?" — Such questions may come from creationists who think the precursor to the eye was some sort of half-assembled eye, as though biology was as simple as Lego. This argument is so illogical that it's worth learning a bit about the eye to refute it properly. For instance, the human eye is far from perfect — while human vision is based on only three colors, some birds and fish can see up to five; we have poor underwater and night vision; and we can't see ultraviolet, infra-red and polarized light, while some animals can. Furthermore, our eyes can't function for long in the vacuum of space without a spacesuit, which, among the other human frailties, will be a hindrance during space exploration.

Apart from these and other avenues for future improvement, we also know of many animals today that have worse eyesight — indeed, we have discovered pretty much all of those "intermediate" forms alive right at this very moment, starting from a patch of cells that can detect light, to the pinhole camera of the nautilus.[1]

How did humans evolve from monkeys, given that there are still monkeys?

Humans did NOT evolve from the monkeys that we see around us today. We may, however, consider ourselves distant cousins with them. Rather, we and the "monkeys" we see today share a common ancestry that is measured in the tens of millions of years. This question is like asking, "If humans evolved from mammals, why are there still mammals?" It is not your job to teach people biology. If you do hear such a response, it is most likely coming from a creationist, and you will not be able to "educate" someone who has managed to tune out all the information they've already been exposed to. The best you can do is direct that poor person to National Geographic, the "Nature" series (still available on the Internet) and other resources, if he seems open to a little self-education, and gracefully exit.

---

[1] http://en.wikipedia.org/wiki/Evolution_of_the_eye

What are the chances of humans evolving without divine intervention?

The chances that humans had of evolving are astronomically slim — indeed so low as to be negligible. However, so are the chances of the giraffe evolving and having that long neck, or the blue whale, which is the largest animal alive.

Looking at the question that way is simply not productive. It is not the atheist who is saying we were pre-determined to turn out this way. We could easily not have evolved, and the giraffe could also not have existed. However, the niche that the giraffe currently exploits — being able to live in hot climates and being tall enough to eat the leaves from tall trees, might have been exploited by some other animal that adapted to that environment — it might be "giraffe-like," with long legs and neck, or it might fly to eat those leaves, or it might jump really high onto those trees, or it might be short but be able to stretch itself into something tall when it is near trees. In the same way, the human being became successful by exploiting its own biological niches and being able to survive in more and more habitats through ingenuity and intelligence. It is not a given that if humans were to not exist, then some other, similarly intelligent species would have taken their place.

People that ask this question also imply that humans are the "final, fully evolved, the end-product of evolution." This is also false of course: even humans are gradually evolving, and over millions of years we will look slightly different, but in tens or hundreds, assuming humanity survives that long, we will be unrecognizable.

I still can't accept evolution — there are no transitional forms.

This is both false and has within it a lack of understanding of how the scientific process works; there are tons of fossils of the species that led up to humans, which gives us a pretty good understanding of how we evolved.[1]

However, there is a tactic that is used here, when people are not arguing in good faith (seeking to find out what is true) but are defending their beliefs. When presented with a fossil showing a transitional form between two species, the believer will then ask for the transitional fossils in between those, and if and when that such are shown, further transitional fossils will be asked for — he will never be satisfied. While the more fossils we have the better, we do not need every single one of them to know that we and chimps share a common ancestor, and that both of us evolved from old-world monkeys — the fossils that we do have provide compelling snapshots of the various stages in our evolution, and while it would be cool to have the full video, we can be already pretty satisfied with what we currently are in possession of.

---

[1] As always, Wikipedia is your friend: http://en.wikipedia.org/wiki/List_of_transitional_fossils#Human_evolution

Exercise Time! (Creationism)

Think up a brief response:
1. The eye is too complex to have evolved naturally — what good is half an eye?
2. Why are there still monkeys if the human being is the ultimate product of evolution?
3. There are no transitional forms between humans and apes.

THE GIST OF ISLAM

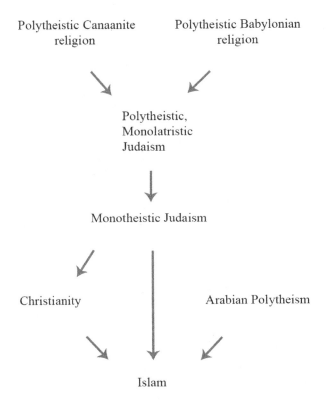

Much to the chagrin of fundamentalist Christians, Islam is not some weird alien religion but is actually very closely related to Judaism and Christianity. Muslims believe in much of the Judeo-Christian lore, like Adam and Eve, Noah and the flood, and even that Jesus existed and was a prophet. (However, Muslims do not believe that he was God incarnate.)

The general Muslim view regarding the Jews and Christians is that they used to have a pure version of the faith (the one that the Muslims now possess) but that it became corrupted over time. If anything, the Muslims hold more closely to Old Testament values, although they do not follow the Torah/Tanakh/Bible per se. Muslims however "revere" them, or more specifically what they consider their "original" versions, since they have now become "corrupted" and the current versions are not to be trusted. According to some interpretations of Islam, you can actually be Jewish or Christian and still get to heaven since you still believe in the one and only God.

While we do not have proof that Jesus actually lived, we do know that Muhammad did indeed exist, for his deeds were interwoven with historical events, and he left behind a large heritage and many descendants.

Islam is often presented as meaning "peace"; however, the true meaning is "surrender." While reading the Quran, I found it was much more coherent than the Bible, which by comparison is a disjointed group of writings. The Quran is more like something that someone with a unified agenda might come up with. It is unclear how true to the original variant the current Qurans are. Prophet Muhammad himself was illiterate, and preached to his followers, who would ostensibly either record the information themselves or pass it on to people who would. The Quran was first transcribed using a system of writing which could be viewed as a predecessor to the current Islamic/Arabic writing system, which was very error-prone and open to interpretation depending on the shape of the strokes. It is also unclear which parts have been added later and simply attributed to Muhammad to suit the later leaders' agendas. The "strictness and harshness" of the Quran increases towards the end. While many Muslim apologists search the Quran for more diplomatic quotes to appease people during debates, it is actually the later verses that are more intolerant which today hold more weight with Muslim scholars.

Arabian Polytheism influences in Islam

You may have noticed that there is an "Arabian Polytheism" branch in the Islamic history chart at the beginning of this chapter. Muhammad came from a polytheistic background — there is a large black cube in Mecca that Muslims circle during the Hajj (it's called the Kaaba), which used to be dedicated to the god Hubal and contained various Idols to different deities of that pantheon.

Muhammad's grandfather almost sacrificed Muhammad's father to Hubal. From Ibn Hisham:

An arrow showed that it was 'Abdullah to be sacrificed. 'Abdul-Muttalib then took the boy to Al-Ka'bah with a razor to slaughter the boy. Quraish, his uncles from Makhzum tribe and his brother Abu Talib, however, tried to dissuade him. They suggested that he summon a she-diviner. She ordered that the divination arrows should be drawn with respect to 'Abdullah as well as ten camels. ... the number of the camels (finally) amounted to one hundred. ... They were all slaughtered to the satisfaction of Hubal

Indeed, the "Arabian Polytheism," as I've labeled it, may actually have its roots or have been influenced by the ancient Mesopotamian polytheism.

The people of that region were often at war, but once a year all of those folks agreed to a truce and went to Mecca for religious ceremonies relating to the Kaaba.

Allah was not invented by Muhammad, and existed as part of the Arabic pantheon, analogous to the way in which Yahweh existed in the Canaanite pantheon prior to becoming a monotheistic type of god. The ancient Meccans considered Allah as the creator god and giver of rain, and he had many sons and daughters who were also divinities. If any Islamic apologists don't believe you, note that Muhammad's father's name literally means "slave of Allah," which would mean that either his grandfather had great foresight into his son's future religion, or Allah did indeed exist as part of a pantheon prior to being made the one and only god. [1]

The Rise of Islam

Muhammad used to be a pretty ordinary man from Mecca — he started of earning a living as a shepherd, and was later married to his first wife, Khadija, who was a successful merchant, and did some business relating to trading. He also spent several weeks of the year in a cave meditating. It was during one of those meditations that the angel Gabriel supposedly appeared to him, and asked him to recite some verses about how God created man, how God taught man and overall how awesome God was:

> Proclaim! (or read!) in the name of thy Lord and Cherisher, Who created-
> Created man, out of a (mere) clot of congealed blood:
> Proclaim! And thy Lord is Most Bountiful,-
> He Who taught (the use of) the pen,-
> Taught man that which he knew not
> —Quran, sura 96

Anyhow after Muhammad heard Angel Gabriel for the first time, according to some sources he was quite disconcerted, fearing that he may be crazy.[2] He initially was reluctant to speak about it, and went to his wife Khadija, who was actually quite enthusiastic about the whole thing.

He started preaching in Mecca (which, remember, at the time was a polytheistic city). Now, what makes this story believable to me is that after he started preaching his views and bashing the old religious order, the people of the town first mocked him, but as the veracity of his speeches increased,

---

[1] http://en.wikipedia.org/wiki/Arabian_mythology
[2] He "feared that the revelation experience was an evil touch preying upon him, playing with him mentally, upsetting his tranquility and peace of mind." http://www.al-islam.org/restatement-history-islam-and-muslims-sayyid-ali-ashgar-razwy/birth-islam-and-proclamation-muhammad

they became angry and threw him out of the city (the story could have easily been that everyone in the city was very impressed and instantly embraced his teachings). He was exiled along with a few people who became his followers, who believed him.

After a while he ended up in Medina, where there was a lot of infighting. Since he was an outsider, he was somehow appointed as an "arbiter" and after a while became quite influential. His forces grew, and eventually he became so powerful as to overthrow the peoples in Mecca who initially drove him out of town. He then threw all of the polytheistic statues and what not out of the Kaaba and made it Islam-only. This made a lot of people very upset I presume. He continued on to conquer and rule many more territories in Arabia, and created some degree of unity in that region.

Then there are the Jinn. Those are spiritual, invisible beings that can also interact with physical objects (don't ask me how that works). They were created after the angels but before humans. The Jinn can be good, bad or neutral, just like people. If you've seen "Aladdin" then you might be familiar with the "Genie" — the two are more or less synonyms, however according to Islamic lore they are invisible, also they are usually not trapped in lamps and are not so cartoony — in fact, in the age before Islam they used to be worshipped in their own right. To recap, the Jinn are spiritual beings akin to ghosts (but they were never actually people), that used to be worshipped, then became side-characters in Islam, and later became side-characters in Disney cartoons.

Many Muslims still believe in Jinn to this day, in the same way that some Christians believe in demons and ghosts: I've heard accounts of it being taken to such an extreme that, if, say, the wind blew and hence a door slammed shut, or if something fell off the table, it would be instantly (and in seemingly complete seriousness) be proclaimed that "A Jinn did it!"

The 5 pillars of Islam

(1) Testimony:
  "I bear witness that there are no deities other than Allah alone and I testify that Muhammad is his Messenger."
(2) Prayer:
  Pray 5 times a day.
(3) Alms-giving:
  Give to charity (usually 2.5% yearly, more is urged from the rich).
(4) Fasting:
  No food from sunrise to sunset during the month of Ramadan.
(5) Pilgrimage (Hajj):
  Go to Mecca at least once in your lifetime.

Islam has its own system of laws (Judaism and Christianity do as well, though we rarely hear about that today), and many Muslim-majority countries have attempted to implement them to some degree at the national level. There is no distinction between religious and state matters under those laws. Islam is both a religion and a political ideology.

Islamic norms and customs

This list will be far from exhaustive — you understand there are many more:

1. Pork. Muslims and Jews are taught that pigs are dirty ("unclean") animals. This originated from the Hebrew prohibitions on eating pork. Eating pork is forbidden in the book of Leviticus.

2. Veil. All proper Muslim women who are "of age" are taught to wear the veil. There is no real description of what that should look like in the Quran, beyond the notion that "women have to be modest and cover themselves." Interpretations vary from the liberal headscarf to the full body covering with eye-holes.

3. Alcohol. Alcohol is "Haram" (forbidden) due to it distancing you from God. If you die while intoxicated, you could go to Hell. However, historically this was not always the case.

4. Circumcision. Ouch, now that really hurts. This is also taken from Judaism, but here sometimes women are circumcised as well. Muslims, Jews, and many Christians have notions about why circumcision is a good thing, however I speculate this has more to do with belonging to a group: the higher the cost of joining a group, the more loyal the members; American university fraternities use the same general principle in the form of hazing.

5. Dancing. Depending on the region, dancing may be okay, may be frowned upon, or may get you stoned to death. In Sufi Islam, however, spinning around till you get dizzy is actually a part of religious practice.

The death of Muhammad and the split of Islam into Sunni and Shia

After Muhammad's death, it quickly became apparent that, even though he was "The last Prophet" and everybody agreed on that, the question of succession still had to be made — since leadership decisions still had to be done. The people who became Shia Muslims believed that the leadership role should be hereditary, and should stay within the prophet's family. The Sunnis, on the other hand, believed that the leader should be chosen. These two groups then sat down, discussed their differences, and found the gap unbridgeable. There has been intermittent animosity between these two groups ever since, but in most regions they have been coexisting like the Protestants and Catholics, with only the occasional slaughter here and there.

Since Prophet Muhammad's sayings were vague regarding the method of choosing a successor (the Sunni route), throughout history various ways have been improvised, including elections by the Muslim community, nominations by the existing leader and selection by a small group of higher-ups.

Wahabi Islam, the Kharijites and the Taliban

Before the Sunni and Shia split, not long after the death of Muhammad, the Kharijites came into being — they did not recognize the authority of Caliphs, and were the most hardcore group of Islamists one could find. They didn't last long. However, a long time after their destruction a new movement called Wahabi Islam emerged and is now the mainstream ideology in Saudi Arabia. However Saudi Arabia's recent prosperity, education and international exposure have led to moderation, and most Muslims now reject the ideas that Wahabi Islam proclaimed hundreds of years ago.

The overwhelming majority of Muslims, just like everyone else, are generally peaceful and care more about their jobs, family and friends rather than "waging war on the West."

Additional Resources:
- The Quran
- *The Complete Infidel's Guide to the Koran* by Robert Spencer
- "The Jinn And Tonic Show" (online show)

ISLAMIC COUNTER-APOLOGETICS

Islam has a lot of apologetics similar to Christianity, and prior to reading this chapter I recommend the "Counter-Apologetics" chapter. This chapter will focus on Islam-specific arguments.

Islam is the religion of peace.

Not quite. If we were to rank religions according to peacefulness, Jainism would have to be victorious, since there the devout are afraid of hurting insects, so they swipe in front of their feet as they walk, and wear surgical masks to avoid perchance inhaling a fly or mosquito. A fundamentalist follower of Jainism would possibly be the safest person to be around.

Indeed, the concept of Islam being the religion of peace works only if the entire world is Muslim, and furthermore, of a single sect of Islam — then there can be Islamic "peace." I do not negate, of course, the fact that the vast majority of Muslims are peaceful, kind and good human beings, just as not all Brits were megalomaniacs that wanted to take over other peoples' territories. However, as Sam Harris put it, "The problem with Islamic fundamentalism are the fundamentals of Islam."[1]

---

[1] Sam Harris's speech regarding "The problem with Islamic fundamentalism are the fundamentals of Islam." http://www.youtube.com/watch?v=vDMOxjHIt0U

The Quran and the Hadiths do contain many violent and hateful statements.[1] But the Quran never actually says to "kill nonbelievers." That is in the Hadiths.

To be fair, the Bible contains around twice as many "evil" quotes."[2]

Some Islamic apologists will give the argument that depending on the chronology of the verses, some are more important and "overrule" other verses; however that is just cherry-picking, like Christians claiming that the violence in their book doesn't count, since it's in the Old Testament, all the while still using the Ten Commandments which are taken from the Old Testament.

The overwhelming majority of Muslims are far more moral than the Quran, and they live peaceful and productive lives. So are most Christians and Jews, who do not stone witches, adulterers, gays or followers of other faiths, even though their holy books explicitly tell them to do so.

The Quran is scientific/compatible with science.

Muslim apologists will often mention that the Quran has scientific knowledge in it which could not have been known by humans of that period. This includes fields such as embryology and geology. However, the ancient Greeks of that time had MUCH more knowledge than what was contained in the Quran, and a lot of the "science" in the Quran is faulty: embryos are described as "blood clots" and mountains supposedly have roots.

Quotes in the Quran are usually quite vague, and the scientific knowledge miracles that the apologists profess require a lot of "interpretation." Indeed, while the Quran doesn't specifically say that "the earth is flat," it can be inferred from phrases such as "we spread out the earth" that it was assumed at the time that the earth was indeed flat.

The Quran is a literally and linguistic miracle.

One common Islamic apologetic is that the Quran is a perfect work of literature, indeed a "miracle," because no other work comes close and humans by themselves could not have come up with something so beautiful. This claim then goes on to explain all of the intricacies of the way the Quran is written and how this is impossible for humans to create.[3]

[1] Quote-mining the Quran for evil stuff, http://www.skepticsannotatedbible.com/quran/cruelty/long.html
[2] Comparison between the evil quotes in the Quran and the Bible, http://dwindlinginunbelief.blogspot.com/2006/06/which-is-more-violent-bible-or-quran.html
[3] The Quran as a linguistic and literally miracle argument, http://www.hamzatzortzis.com/essays-articles/exploring-the-quran/the-inimitable-quran/

But such apologists are comparing the Quran to itself. The same logic can be found around proud parents, who consider their little rascal to be the incarnation of Albert Einstein and Michael Jordan combined. Indeed, if you were raised around the Quran, told to learn it by heart, recite it, and such, and have a peer group that deeply respects it, then of course you are going to think it is a masterpiece — that's how culture works. To say otherwise would be blasphemy — like a British person saying he thinks Shakespeare was not that good a poet. One could as well suggest that albums by 2Pac and Biggie Smalls are miracles of the rap world, since to this day no rapper has been able to come close.

I have read the English version of the Quran, and was only slightly more impressed with it than with the Bible. Its main advantage is that there is at least a semblance of a general aim, and of some "point" that the author was trying to make, as opposed to the chaotic nature of the Bible. No doubt some Muslims will suggest I should learn Quranic Arabic and read it in its original language. True, it may be more beautiful in the original, but shouldn't an "ultimate written work," transmitted by an omnipotent being, be beautiful and coherent when translated into any language?

The Quran is Inimitable

Chances are, you will be told that "The Quran is Inimitable," meaning that "no human can create anything similar or 'like it'" — therefore it could only have come from God. No doubt an expert in Classical Arabic could come up with something — however, who is the "judge" of what constitutes "inimitable"? Islamic "experts" will no doubt reject it because it is not the Quran. Inimitable is a tricky concept — I actually have no problem admitting that the Quran is "inimitable," but then so are snowflakes, songs, my fingerprint and any book you can pick up off the shelf.

We are also faced with the issue that the challenge is described in several different ways:

> "Were all mankind to come together and wish to produce the like of the Qur'an, they would never succeed, however much they aided each other".
> (17:88)

> *"Or do they say: 'He forged it'? Say: 'Bring then a sura like unto it and call anyone you can".*
> *(10:38)*

> *"Do people imagine that this Qur'an is not from Us, and that you, O Prophet are falsely attributing to us? Tell them that if they are speaking truly they should produce ten surahs resembling the Qur'an, and that they are free to call on the aid of anyone but God in so doing." (11:13)*

The Quran is written in "pure" Arabic.

No language is "pure." All languages borrow from other languages; that's how they grow. Indeed, the Quran is not "pure." For example:

In the Quran, the word "Injil" means "gospel" and "good news." However, there is a perfectly fine Arabic word for that which is "bisharah." On the other hand, "Injil" is derived from either Greek or Aramaic.

The Quran uses the word "Pharaoh," which means king in Egyptian. In Arabic there is a different word for "King."

There are no contradictions in the Quran.

The Quran, just like the Bible, is full of contradictions, as a five-second Google search will reveal. But note how irrelevant this argument is: if I were to write a story with no contradictions, this would not make the story true.

Islam is the oldest religion

According to this view, the Christianity and Judaism of today are "corrupted versions" of that original religion, which Prophet Muhammad restored. This argument ignores the existence of other older belief systems that pre-date Judaism (roughly 1500 BCE[1]), be it Hinduism[2] (roughly 3300

[1] http://en.wikipedia.org/wiki/Jewish_history
[2] It is a simplification on my part, for the sake of brevity, to call the religion(s)

BCE) or the array of now-extinct polytheistic religions. Also, if you consult the handy chart at the beginning of the chapter "The Gist of Islam" you will notice that Judaism evolved from polytheistic religions, where Yahweh (now conflated with Allah) was part of a pantheon of gods. The notion of monotheism was a much later innovation. If this argument is true, then it renders invalid the core notion of Islam, that:

> *"There is no god but God, Muhammad is the messenger of God."*

The Quran is perfect.

For this you don't even need to search out contradictions or know any verses, it is all much simpler, and can be refuted in these 4 easy steps:

1. Muhammad is the messenger of Allah, and the Quran is the message/revelation from Allah.

2. The purpose of a message is to relay knowledge/information.

3. If a message requires additional information/explanation/context/interpretation to be fully understood, then it is not a perfect message.

4. The Quran requires the Hadith to be fully understood, so the Quran is not perfect.

The argument you shouldn't use

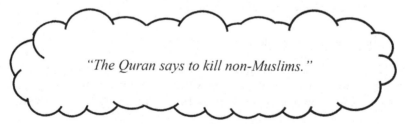

"The Quran says to kill non-Muslims."

Wrong. I myself have read the Quran, expecting to find verses to that effect. While there are many verses deploring unbelievers and saying that they will go to Hell, there is no overt command to kill them. The more extreme parts are in the Hadith:

---

of the Indus Valley of 3300 BCE "Hinduism" — the beliefs of that region have a quite long and complicated history, which you can read up on. I use "Hinduism" as an umbrella term to encompass the belief systems of that region.

> *"I have been ordered to fight with the people till they say, none has the right to be worshipped but Allah."*
> *-Al Bukhari vol 4:196.*

Even this is usually explained away by most Muslim apologists as "applying only in times of war." And "fight" can mean many things, including debate, which we consider a better approach. There are some contradicting verses as well which talk about peace, and how Islam prohibits killing and suicide. For most people, I would recommend staying away from this argument as it can easily be turned against you.

Exercise Time! (Islamic Counter-Apologetics)

Think up a brief response:
1. Islam promotes peace.
2. Stop being Islamophobic and respect Islam!
3. The Quran is an inimitable literally miracle!

> Additional Resources:
> - *A Manual for Creating Atheists* by Peter Boghossian
> - "The Atheist Experience" (online show)
> - "The Jinn And Tonic Show" (online show)
> - "The Magic Sandwich Show" (online show)
> - "The Thinking Atheist" (online show)

THE PROTECTIVE INNER MEASURES OF THE BELIEVER

In the chapter on "Paralogic Compliance," I in part talked about how the mind does its best to keep a single coherent worldview. This occurs at a price; however, since we sometimes ignore or rationalize away inconvenient facts: even with a normally-functioning brain, this is sometimes observable. People who are particularly adept at the art of ignoring inconvenient facts may be labeled obstinate or even republican.

In *Phantoms of the Brain*, V.S. Ramachandran describes how some paralyzed patients will confabulate, rationalize away and downright deny their predicament. When asked to move their paralyzed arm and touch the doctor's nose, they made such excuses as "I don't like taking orders," "I have severe arthritis," "I am using that hand for balance," or downright "I am within an inch of your nose" (they weren't). The reason that this does not occur to such an obvious degree in healthy individuals is that we have a "balance of power," if you will, in our brains: there is a part in one hemisphere which makes all of these excuses. However there is also another part, in the other hemisphere, whose role it is to raise questions, and so most of the time we have a respectable truce. In those patients where this occurs, however, the part that is supposed to help identify things that don't make sense is damaged, and so the excuse-making, confabulating and rationalizing part is given free license to run free and do all it wants to keep the person's worldview the same. When prodded further and further, some of these patients actually became aware of the fact that they were paralyzed, sometimes causing emotional outbursts. However, a bit later, they could no longer remember their realizations. Also, when some patients regained the use of their paralyzed parts, they did not remember saying that they were previously able to move them and "re-wrote" their memories, making them believe that they always acknowledged that they were unable to move their arms back when they were paralyzed.

Does the same thing occur with religious minds? Not exactly, but this example above can serve as a useful illustration as to why some of them may seem so obstinate in the face of information that should have made a "reasonable religious person" into an atheist ages ago. Also, I should say that this varies greatly from person to person: some believers, for instance, never had access to information that challenged their worldview, or never really bothered to think much about it.

Be that as it may, with your typical "devout believer" the defense mechanisms become instantly recognizable. We dealt with counter-apologetics in the previous chapters — this chapter is not about answering specific arguments that believers might throw at you, but about why such illogical arguments are presented in the first place, and why some believers will simply ignore their previous defeat in a discussion and it will be as if that discussion never happened or they remembered it differently, as if they were living in a different reality from us rational people. While some may attribute this to mere debate tactics, and that the believers really "know" that they actually lost a debate, or things like that, and while that may sometimes be the case with professional debaters, I argue that most do sincerely believe in what they are professing, and actually "see things differently," since their actual perceptions of discussions, logic, events are all shaped to conform to their worldviews. Indeed, this is not limited to religious folk — all of us do this, and without this we would be unable to function. The difference is that some recognize this fact and try to have as few false beliefs as possible, while others are blissfully ignorant.

With this, we will now visit a controversial subject, Freud. Never mind his notions about sex, his other contribution is more useful — the notion that our consciousness is not some magical thing that comes from a soul but is an end result of a physical process, and is an elaborate illusion that we strive to protect at all costs. For this we utilize a number of defense mechanisms, and I hypothesize that the believing mind uses those same processes to cling onto its worldview. I will list of these classical defense mechanisms that Freud first came up with, and add atheism-related examples.

Denial:
> *No, I did not lose my one million dollars!*
> *There is no way I am going to die from this cancer!*
> *What those atheists say about God is total BS; they are just demon-worshippers.*

Repression:
> This occurs when people have admitted to some points in a debate, or perhaps have seen conclusive evidence that should overturn their worldview, however, they conveniently ignore or forget all this.

Reaction Formation:
> In layman's terms this is "overcompensation." For instance, some of the most "anti-gay" folks act extremely macho, but turn out to have homosexual tendencies. I argue that we sometimes see the same trend in the most overtly devout believers — these outer displays of religiosity may sometimes be attributed to an inner doubt, regarding which they are compensating.

Rationalization:
> "Well, Noah was able to build that large ark because the angels helped him, and after the flood the different animals walked to their respective continents via special 'land bridges' which are now gone."

Humor:
> (In response to criticism of genital mutilation/circumcision)
> "Statistically, the only long term effect that circumcision has on people is it increases their chances of winning the Nobel Prize." (This is a real point that was made by a rabbi in a debate with the late Christopher Hitchens[1])

Projection:
> "You atheists are so angry!"[2]
> "You can lead an atheist to evidence but you can't make him think" (this is actually a title of a book by Ray Comfort).

Now, the risk that one runs is one begins viewing every single thing believers say through these Freudian lenses — this is not my intent: there

---

[1] The circumcision joke and Hitchen's reply: http://www.youtube.com/watch?v=Xx_ov2NiNo4
[2] Granted, some atheists are angry, but often this is used as a projection when the believer gets angry in response to the arguments an atheist makes and assumes that these arguments were made with anger in mind.

are believers out there whom you can reason out of their beliefs, and there are those who simply don't care. However, this is an important tool to have, as it may help you diagnose occurrences of these in your discussions. When you are sure about your "diagnosis" and you are running in circles around the same topic, calmly but bluntly point those out, as in:

"Jake, I think you are projecting — I am not really angry. Perhaps, however, the things I've said angered you? Why is that?"

"I think your use of humor is an avoidance tactic that you're using instead of dealing with what I've said — may we discuss it further?"

"I think there are some doubts behind your overt displays of religiosity — if it's not a secret, may I ask if you are using that to compensate?"

"We discussed this issue some time ago and resolved it; I feel as if you are conveniently forgetting it."

Such overt call-outs may elicit anger, an "honest" response, or perhaps nothing at all. But hey, at least you tried and stayed true to yourself. Repeatedly call these out when you see them, but be absolutely sure — one false diagnosis and you'll run the risk of being labeled a pseudo-psychologist (or indeed, even if you are correct and your point is especially salient, some people will use such comments as a defense mechanism to attempt to disarm you)

Sam: "You're just playing psychoanalyst — please stop that, it's silly."

Jack: "Right, but is there some truth to what I have said?"

NEAR-DEATH EXPERIENCES PROVE NOTHING

There are numerous marvelous stories of people coming out of surgery, sometimes in which their hearts even stopped beating, and reporting of having been "in heaven" (or sometimes in hell). This sure is a great way to attract TV viewers and "increase their faith." What better "proof" could we ask for?

There are, of course, several major problems with this.

Let's think about the practice of "Sleep Induction." There is a practice known as lucid dreaming (inducing controlled dreams where you know you are dreaming). A common way of inducing the dreams is to repeat what you want to happen in the dream over and over as you are falling asleep, and imagine it as vividly as possible. Now, if we take that concept and transfer it to a hospital where, say, a devout Catholic thinks he may die in the next few hours — I wonder what will be on his mind? Chances are, he will be praying constantly and having religious thoughts. It is no surprise that he may just experience such a dream under anesthesia, and this could indeed happen relatively often. When combined with the propensity of the media to pick up on such stories and ignore stories of people seeing the Easter

Bunny instead, it is then indeed expected that we'd hear a lot of such reports. And it always seems that the religious imagery visualized by the person in question is in accordance with her cultural background and religious views. We never seem to witness, for instance, a Christian fundamentalist seeing Muhammad and Allah in heaven, having him renounce his religious views and become a devout Muslim.

THOUGHTS ON BUDDHISM

Initially, when compared to the more widespread and easier to criticize religions, Buddhism may seem like the sort of "just let it slide" type of religion, and indeed, I'd much prefer to live in a society that is full of Buddhists rather than Christians or Muslims.

However, Buddhism contains frustrating implications which, I dare say, are simply not true. For instance, there is a strong notion that one should never entertain negative emotions and should strive to avoid them at all costs. If a person does experience them, it somehow diminishes the person's spiritual progress. Buddhism espouses the absolute disdain of such things as alcohol, sexual pleasure, adrenaline or anything seemingly exciting, since they would drive you off the correct path. The seemingly benign notion of karma is toxic. It may sound fair, at first — that "people get what they deserve," but it can lead to inaction. Suffering can be seen as a sort of "karma replenishment" tool — many Buddhists assume that the suffering they are undergoing now will somehow be repaid with benefits later on, and conversely if they see someone else suffering, then it is their karma and they deserved it.

If the notions of reincarnation, of the different world types that exist in Buddhism, and of Nirvana were accurate, then Buddhism would be an invaluable resource for attaining Nirvana. Buddhism does have some very insightful things to say about how humans think and behave and can be considered one of the first attempts at a systematic psychology. However, the problem is that the premise is wrong, and as such, the whole thing falls apart.

For one thing, all suffering, perhaps with some rare exceptions that help you grow as a human being and build character, is generally bad and meaningless. Buddhism promotes being strong on the inside while enduring everything that is bad, while saying that by no means should you cause anyone else the least bit of suffering, for that will give you bad karma. It is of course not stated in those terms, but those are its implications.

In effect, this can cause you to almost become an emotional (or even physical) punching bag for others who do not follow the same rules — Buddhists can be too "mild and meek" to fight back, allowing others to take advantage of them. This is of course not true for all schools of Buddhism and people can be unique, but this is how I saw it.

If you take away the Nirvana and the reincarnation it now seems that

Buddhism has you chasing fools' gold: while anger, alcohol consumption, sex can be harmful if not done with the proper precautions, and these teachings probably were quite a useful guide for the people that lived thousands of years ago, and while many people still live "in harmony" in accordance to Buddhism, I simply feel that it has too much toxic baggage to be more than a "passing phase" religious people take on their way to atheism — it can be useful to experience it for a short while, and I was fortunate as a child to actually believe many of those things — I do believe it can be beneficial in terms of character-building, but only up to a point — once I started maturing, learning more about critical thinking, and reading books about how the mind works, atheism, psychology and the like, I was more than happy to free myself from this now tightening garment I used to think was the truth.

Ironically, only now that I am free from the supernatural worldview of Buddhism was I finally able to more or less attain the happiness and ease of mind that it promised. I realized that it's OK to get angry every once in a while, and to be unapologetic about it, and to live life to the fullest. Buddhism on the other hand considers anger toxic, without much room for nuance.[1] I shudder to think that I could have lived this life without the without the adrenaline-inducing skydives, bungee jumps, and the other thrills of life. Furthermore, my character would still be of the mild kind, rather than the more assertive go-getting kind that I am currently developing. Buddhism still has a soft spot for me, since I find that the techniques to keep calm and have a centered and stable worldview that is not as affected by outside occurrences still works, and is of great benefit — and indeed, there are many "atheistic Buddhists" out there, that reject the supernatural parts of Buddhism and just adhere to the Buddhist philosophy. But Buddhism does not hold a monopoly on "being calm, centered and in control of your emotions" — which are the good qualities that it helped me develop.

Another negative effect of the belief in karma and reincarnation is that it gets people to worrying about what they might have done or experienced in a past life. We have enough trouble dealing responsibly with one life at a time.

NO MORE DIVINE KINGS

The separation of Church and State is such a new concept that it would have seemed bizarre to anyone living earlier in history. The notion that the rulers are also the spiritual leaders goes back to the first human settlements. While nomadic people did have religions and rituals, the notion of a "Divine King" began to emerge only once people became farmers. The move from hunter-gathering to being stationary and growing your own crops meant that you no longer had to worry that much about dying of hunger or being eaten by lions. You had all of the commodities of someone in the third world today: bread, meat, a warm place to sleep, and plentiful beer-like beverages. Initially,

---

[1] http://www.accesstoinsight.org/lib/authors/piyatissa/bl068.html

people who were farmers were at a disadvantage: they would constantly be raided by people who spent more or less their entire free time perfecting their killing skills. After a while, however, the raiders began to realize that it wasn't quite profitable to raid and kill everyone, since there would be no one to raid during next harvest season. They began to "raid and take a bit and not kill everyone." Then multiple gangs began competing. Eventually, the initial "raiding warlords" became the "protectors" of the people — this is how the first armies and kings appeared. This is of course a gross oversimplification, and the first sedentary (non-nomadic) communities of various regions have their own distinct formation histories.

A strong kingdom can only exist if the people truly respect the king and are ready to die for him. What better way to ensure this than to make him divine? If a king is in the lineage of the gods, then his commands are beyond question. I doubt there was a "conspiracy" to fool the people, but rather this notion of the "Divine King" might have evolved numerous times in various cultures simply because it was the most evolutionarily successful. The "divine right of Kings" was recognized in ancient Egypt, Rome, medieval Europe, in Japan, China, Tibet and other parts of Asia. It was only after people became literate that they understood they were being had. As such, the previous "environment" that supported the divinity of kings was now actively being destroyed through education, literacy and new political ideas. In the next chapter I will argue that just as the "environment" that allowed kings to exist is now more or less gone, today the environment that allows religions themselves to exist and for new large-scale religions to be created is now actively being destroyed as well.

WHEN WILL RELIGIONS JUST GO AWAY?

Religions may never completely vanish from our societies, since the very things that make us human also make us susceptible to religious indoctrination (see "Why do humans believe?"). On the other hand, religion for the most part is already losing its grip on the more educated and well-off societies (the United States and United Arab Emirates being some notable counterexamples), and being confined to more symbolic, metaphorical and ceremonial roles such as marriage and funeral ceremonies.

What we do know, however, is that countries that tend to be highly religious are generally less well-off than their more secularized counterparts — even in the United States, the more religious states are those that have much more crime, unwanted pregnancies, poverty and low education levels. Again, correlation does not equal causation: is it the religious influence that's holding those communities back or is it that the difficult environment that drives people to religion? My firm belief is that the two are feeding off each other, and that only through a heavy dose of education, especially in the areas of science and critical thinking skills, will those communities be able to begin to escape their predicament. Unfortunately the education system in the United States has lost a lot of ground in the last few decades. One must not imagine that "the lack of religiosity and rise of secularism" is an inevitable result, and that societal progress is pre-determined. That would make us no different from religious-minded individuals who assume that, given enough time, the world shall surely see the value of their particular religious views.

Rather, I propose that just as it is possible to see religions as "Memes," "Idea Organisms" or "God Viruses," depending on what you wish to call them, which struggle for survival and try to out-compete each other on the battlefield of ideas, so is Atheism, as an active rejection of that belief, involved in that battle. Many atheists do not share this belief, and give analogies such as "Religions are like collecting stamps, and being an atheist is not collecting stamps," or "Religions are like TV channels and being an atheist is turning off the TV." I consider that too naïve. True, atheism has no central creed or doctrine, and it would be improper to consider it a religion; but neither is the atheism that you possess: "a well thought-out rejection of the religious deities of the world based on the knowledge of those deities and of critical thinking, science, different arguments for/against the existence of gods" the same atheism that a dog might possess, which would be based merely on the complete lack of knowledge of the subject. So, even though people might be atheists for different reasons, whether emotional or logical, and possess a wide variety of knowledge or lack thereof, the atheism that exists in the United States is there as a counter-movement to religion. As such, even though atheists have science and reality on their side, there is still a battle underway to influence the minds of the public, and atheism/secularism has far from won.

With the ever-increasing influence of the Internet and other open-source information there is, however, hope.

It may not seem like it, but we could be on the verge of the total collapse of religions. While religion is still everywhere, especially in the US, do you remember that whole "religions as organisms that evolve" paradigm? Currently over fifty percent of people on the entire planet are associated with Judaism, Christianity or Islam. Even with various denominations/ sects this means that there is a lack of diversity, and as any biologist will tell you that whenever there is a lack of genetic diversity in an ecosystem, the population as a whole becomes vulnerable to sudden changes. In the case of religion this is most likely the invention of the Internet. Whereas just a few hundred years ago, it was easy for a belief system to incubate in a village, town or country since it was uncommon for people to travel very far, these days the type of environment that is necessary for the incubation of new religions is being rapidly destroyed, with literacy and education spreading everywhere. Any new idea that you come across can easily be fact-checked within minutes by using an internet-connected smartphone.

It was never easy for a new religion or sect to gain influence and survive past the first few generations. And today there is no large population group that cannot fact-check religious claims and discuss them online.[1] The era of large new religions sprouting up is over, I think, and is to be replaced with smaller cults and different versions of the current existing religions desperately trying to remain relevant. We have dwindling religious diversity, with "tribal religion" (an anthropologist slang term for "miscellaneous religion") being eradicated and replaced with versions of larger religions, which in turn creates a very un-diverse environment that is ripe for a new plague. Let us hope it will be the "plague" of enlightenment and free-thought.

I do not mean to suggest that religion will die out tomorrow, or even in the next generation: it might take hundreds of years or it may never be fully gone, with cults appearing here and there, and religions becoming ever more diluted or metaphorical. But evolutionarily the large world religions are now living on borrowed time. The new generations are increasingly using the Internet and seeing religion as the outdated vestige that it is. Yay! Now go do something cheerful in light of this new knowledge!

THE FUTURE OF HUMANITY

A disclaimer first: the previous chapters dealt with practical issues and talked about historical events. It is much more difficult to predict the future, and I am nowhere near as arrogant to think that it is a task which can be accomplished in a single chapter or indeed by a single human. Rather, I will talk about a single aspect of the near-future: the possibility that we might get rid of aging sometime soon. Think of this last chapter as a thought experiment and a break from all of the seriousness of the previous chapters.

For whatever reason, when potentially fixable human frailties and illnesses are discussed, such as diabetes, AIDS, or spinal cord injuries, aging seems to get a pass, as if it were somehow different, unavoidable, and "natural." However nothing could be further from the truth: if we go by the criteria of "natural," well then cancer and gonorrhea are also natural, so perhaps those shouldn't be fixed either?

We usually talk about death as being unavoidable. For the vast majority of human existence, that was indeed the case, and thus all of the cultural baggage we have surrounding death tends to "justify" it, as if "it weren't so bad." I've recently read about an interesting psychological phenomenon, where in if people were exposed to something that was merely mildly bad, they actually saw as more bad than something really horrific, such as losing a leg, in the long term, because when something is "really bad," we have psychological self-defense mechanisms that kick in, that would, for instance, allow us to see that lost leg as a new opportunity to read more and finally learn that new computer skill. This sort of response simply fails to kick in when we are merely inconvenienced. I wager that the same thing occurs with

---

[1] Except for the Amish, but they're already taken.

the phenomenon of death — people, thinking it is unavoidable, rationalize it away as something that might even be good, since otherwise it would all be too depressing and we would be stuck forever lamenting our mortality.

There is a good chance however, that aging will be "cured." Advances in science are being made all the time, including the recent experiment where aging was seemingly reversed in mice, and human trials are set to begin in about a year of this writing. In any event, aging is now being attacked on multiple fronts. Aubrey de Grey talks of the "escape velocity" for aging, where if you are below a certain age, science will be able to constantly add additional years to your life, and the advances of science will be such that you will constantly be in the "safe zone" with new innovations being created to repair the damage caused by our metabolism quicker than it can accumulate and cause aging. That being said, as of today there is no pill or therapy you can take that will slow down or stop your aging process — the most you can do today is exercise, eat healthily and avoid dangerous activities to prevent your premature death.

A related field is called "transhumanism." Transhumanists argue that people should be able to improve their bodies and minds through genetic and perhaps mechanical augmentation: for example, you could be muscular without exercise, live and not age and have an immense intellect and creativity. Indeed, we already do this today, starting with simple things such as clothes (artificial fur), glasses (eye augmentations), and all sorts of surgical advances, including artificial eyes that allow people to see, hearing aids, prosthetic arms and legs, and so forth.

I indeed would greatly appreciate an advance that would stop aging. While many would decry it as selfish, in the sense that the earth would become overpopulated or that other people "need to be born" to have a chance to live as well, that is a new area of morality that remains to be examined.

True: scientific advances and the constantly increasing human population will not be without peril. A society where people live indefinitely (don't age), have fewer diseases, but are still vulnerable to things such as moving trucks, would face even more resource scarcity due to population growth. Even with the amount of people we have on this earth today, we would need the resources of four whole earths if everyone were to start consuming as much as today's Americans. At the rate at which humanity keeps increasing in numbers, even with technological breakthroughs in food production, there will be a breaking point.

This leaves us with several possibilities for the future. Humanity might face some sort of global environmental apocalypse where either the biosphere is destroyed entirely and the earth becomes an uninhabitable toxic world, or perhaps today's large-scale societies, which have existed for just a blink of an eye in terms of the overall history of the earth, might disappear as quickly as they appeared, and humans will, after an initial die-off, revert to hunter-gathering in small tribes like we see today on zombie-apocalypse

TV shows, minus the zombies. Another intriguing possibility is that the population of the earth might reach some stable point, such as around 10 billion people, where it will remain. This is not entirely implausible: today more and more people are transitioning from an agrarian lifestyle where the paradigm was "the more kids the better," since progeny are essential when you have large areas of land to farm, to living in cities, where even having a single child is a great economic undertaking. With the transition to city life, the empowerment and education of women increases as well, which will once again undermine the previously deeply-engrained societal notions that women are valued for making babies and cooking food. Finally, if this "self-regulation" doesn't occur, the taboo topic of government policies limiting population growth might need to be discussed.

While a lot of sociological research would have to be done to find the best way, gradually changing people's mindsets would be at the heart of the issue. Families with many children would have to be decried as "old-fashioned", "anti-environmental" and "selfish." People who do not support this view would also be derided, and a catchy term would need to be created — "populationist" is a good candidate — as in "someone who supports the uncontrolled growth of the human population."

Some would view this as "the government limiting our freedoms." However, we no longer keep slaves, nor do we condone cruelty towards animals — those were just some of the "freedoms" of some that damaged the overall good, but now we see those as despicable and regard the people from those times as horrid or selfish. Alas, I do not claim to have a solution for how a society with a non-aging population should work, and hopefully the proper rules of conduct will emerge organically, out of necessity as non-aging becomes more common. I hope that humanity will survive the next few centuries, and that it will still retain the good things that make us proud of being human.

AFTER

As Jared looked up from this book, he noticed that the rain had long since ended, and it was now bright and sunny outside. He paid for the book, and as he was going home he walked with a new-found confidence: sure, the world was still a large and unforgiving physics simulation, but he no longer felt empty or alone. He knew that there were countless people like him and that his new views on life have existed even longer than Christianity, and that he could support his views with arguments from countless brilliant people — some of them ancient and some still alive today.

When he got home, he saw that his parents and some of his acquaintances were sitting there, waiting for him, as if to make an intervention — as though he was an alcoholic or drug addict. As his family and friends began confronting him, trying to get him to take the emotional bait and become a Christian out of guilt or obligation, he no longer responded, for he knew that what they were trying to accomplish was done out of their own insecurities and out of their fear. While it was highly annoying, he knew deep inside that he still loved them all, and that eventually they'd come around, and those of his friends that wouldn't were probably not his friends.

As the months went by, Jared read countless books, from philosophy to biology to popular science. As his knowledge of the universe increased, the previous mental box to which he was confined crumbled away completely: he no longer felt that irrational guilt and the fear of Hell when remembering that he was no longer a Christian. Now he was free, and the world was out there waiting for him.

He decided to try as many things as possible to make up for lost time. Since his deconversion, Jared continually met new and interesting people, traveled the world (or at least went to Atlanta), found a more interesting job, which, while it paid less, was actually satisfying, and met the love of his life, who was also an atheist. Then the big day arrived: he stood there, near the exit, wearing his goggles and helmet, with the wind blowing in his face, and, just like that, and after receiving the go-ahead from his instructors, he jumped out of the airplane.

Printed in the United States
By Bookmasters

.